WHO'S DRIVING THE BUS?

SUE GEE

WHO'S DRIVING THE BUS?

LEADERSHIP AND MANAGEMENT IN A FEW EASY STEPS

SUE GEE

Ashburton Business Books

First published in 2013 by
Ashburton Business Books
an imprint of
Ashburton Publishing Limited
12 Windsor Road
Douglas
Isle of Man IM1 3LB
British Isles

ISBN 978-0-9927272-0-8 (Paperback)
ISBN 978-0-9927272-1-5 (eBook-Kindle)
ISBN 978-0-9927272-2-2 (eBook-ePub)

A CIP catalogue record for this book is available from
the British Library

Printed and bound by CPI Group (UK) Ltd, Croydon, CR0 4YY

For my son Jack

I hope this book supports you on your future leadership journey

I love you

INTRODUCTION
TO THE AUTHOR

I can recall the very first time I encountered this high energy whirlwind affectionately known as the "Gee Force". Even in 2006 it was clear to me that she simply had to write a book.

Should you find yourself anywhere close to Sue's gravitational field you will be drawn in to experience a truly thrilling journey! She possesses an energy that has become an increasingly rare commodity in today's business world. Her persistent drive to achieve more and better by simply setting the bar higher every time and not accepting second best is truly inspiring.

I count myself lucky to have had the good fortune of having Sue Gee as part of my inner circle of trusted strategic advisors to help guide me through the maze of establishing and running a business. Sue has the unique ability to assess any situation from a balanced perspective at a strategic level, and then drill down to find answers in the smallest of details. She is able to motivate and inspire people at all echelons in the business world and it is admirable and truly remarkable to witness her share her vast range of knowledge with people in even the most junior positions.

There is a tremendous confidence in Sue's beliefs, demeanour and attitude that can only come from being a student from the school of hard knocks. There is simply nothing to replace experience at her level.

Over the past few years Sue has applied her rigorous business attitude to the creation of this book. I have seen her through her ups and downs, and it is her persistent and unrelenting determination that saw this project through to the end – in fabulous style! It has been a privilege to have been part of this process.

Terry Van Rhyn,
Managing Director, Ashgrove Marketing

Sue lives in the Isle of Man with her son Jack. She runs her own training and development business which specialises in leadership & management training.

For more details go to:

www.whosdrivingthebus.net
www.tlc.co.im

PREFACE
TICKETS PLEASE

Early in my career I thought that if you had enough drive, gumption, energy, and simply the will to achieve, this would guarantee success. For a while it did, or so I believed. I worked 24/7, did whatever was asked of me, went above and beyond the call of duty and, if I'm honest, expected everyone else to always do the same. As a manager, I believed everyone should work to the standards set – whether they were realistic or not. Everything should have been done yesterday. After all, 'we' were all working towards the same goal, weren't we?

Whatever profession I was in at the time – and I've had a few – we hit whatever target I was given, **so why should leadership really matter?** It's difficult to overstate how much it does, but I simply didn't see it.

I was actually good at my job. I knew all the technical stuff and I could do it standing on my head, so promotion came my way. However, I didn't change; I just carried on in exactly the same way – doing, ordering, and expecting others to do the same, without any thought on my part as to why they should. Terms like 'motivation', 'challenge' and 'personal development' weren't part of my dictionary. I believed them to be what many still do - fluffy words, theories and jargon that don't fit in to our real working lives. I was soon to learn that **the hardest job in the world is leading a team,** and that invaluable lesson came to me because of a coffee machine.

It happened one morning as I was walking past the coffee machine and overheard a conversation. It was about me, or more accurately what my colleagues called me - “the machine”. Got the job done and didn’t care about anyone or anything but myself, only the end result. This realisation shocked me; that description was not how I saw myself. From my naïve, insular perspective, I thought my people – notice ‘my’ people – were with me all the way. I was so efficient, even possibly brilliant, in everything I did and because we achieved our targets I had to be right.

Believe me; the learning curve I found myself on was steep. What I learned is the key to leadership.

Teams and leadership are about ‘we’, not ‘I’.

17 years ago, I started a new chapter in my career and got involved in the training arena. For the past 10 years I have headed up my own training company and our key focus has been leadership and management. This has become my passion. Helping others to learn the lessons that made such a difference to me is a personal privilege, I just hope you learn those lessons much earlier in your career.

I want this book to help you on your journey to discovering that effective leadership can make all the difference to you, your job, your people, and your organisation. I hope it will help explain it in non-management speak for those who have never managed before, and as a refresher for those who have been managing people for many a year. My objective is to keep it short and simple by giving you examples, tips, basic theories, and well-known quotes that will help you take forward what real leadership can mean in real life.

Enjoy

THE BUS

In simple terms, I think of leadership as a bus journey and yourself as the bus driver. When I'm delivering training, I believe that if we can make the learning real (and fun) then it is much easier for delegates to link it back to the world in which we live and work. For me, professional analogies and theories are of no value unless they can be linked back to the workplace. I'm certainly not an academic, as will soon be evidenced. For me it is all about what you are really going to do with the information you have. I now meet many ex-delegates who have taken my metaphor for leadership back to their team members, and all state that it has been much easier to explain the concept of leadership to them. I hope the same works for you.

1.

Before you leave the station make certain **ALL** the team are onboard and want to be! Make certain:

a. That your passion and enthusiasm for the journey doesn't lead you to leave the bus station without your team.

b. That you don't leave too quickly, thinking they are onboard when they actually aren't.

c. That every individual is aware of where they are going and what benefits they, the company, and the team, will gain.

2.

Make certain ALL the team stay onboard (traffic lights, zebra crossings, bus stops, traffic jams, accidents, etc. are all opportunities for people to hop off without you seeing). Be aware:

a. They may lose interest and go home.

b. They may get off and walk to the next bus stop (much slower than the bus).

c. They may just wait for the next bus to come along.

d. They may get off the bus and choose a different form of transport altogether.

3.

As the leader and driver, you need to ensure they get on, stay on, and that you all arrive at the same place at the same time.

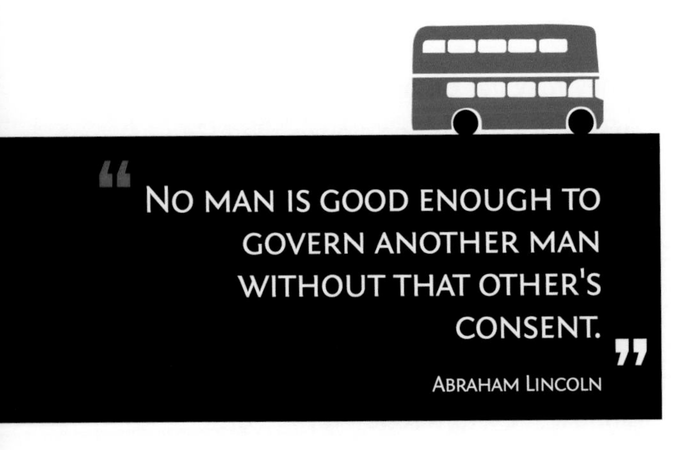

As we explore the different areas of leadership in this book, I will show you what happens to this bus journey if you apply the proper leadership skills - and what can happen if you don't!

CHAPTERS

CHAPTER 1
LEADERSHIP

> “You manage things; you lead people.”
>
> Rear Admiral Grace Murray Hopper

So what do we mean by leadership? Well, it is all about people. Management is about the job, tasks and objectives at hand and leadership is about how willing, knowledgeable, and competent our people are to meet them.

Whereas John Adair (an expert on leadership) looks at it as a combination of individual, task and company needs, **I prefer to look at leadership via a set of scales.** Our job as managers is to balance these scales, with job/task/objective on one side and the needs of our people on the other. The world we live in today requires all of us to have a greater skill set across a broader range of disciplines and in an increasingly fast-changing environment. More often than not, this means chasing deadlines, moving goal posts, and trying to do 10 hours' work in 7. So guess what happens to the scales.

Yes: more focus/weight is loaded on to the job/task/objective side. While this will work for a short period of time, it won't in the long term:

> **people expect more and meeting these expectations is what I mean by leadership.**

The bottom line is that every person who works for you is a **volunteer.** Ultimately, it is they who decide how hard they work and how much commitment they are willing to give to the organisation.

Increasingly, the expectation of staff is that managers will lead rather than drive. That's why, when training on leadership and management, one of the first things I ask my delegates to do is list the key things they expect from a line manager. Here are some examples of words and phrases that appear on those lists every time, and what your staff will expect from you.

To be open, honest, trustworthy; to challenge/ stretch them; to offer them development; to lead by example; to have influencing skills; to stand up for the team; to communicate and share information; to motivate and empower; to be flexible; to offer praise and give feedback; to be helpful and supportive; to make them feel valued.

This list is not exhaustive by any means, but it gives an important insight into what our team members actually look for in a leader. All of the above are about how leaders should behave, how staff are treated, and how they feel about their line manager and their work. Taking this back to the scales, we can't concentrate on the management side without being equally attentive to the team.

CREATE THE CULTURE

Leaders set the tone, which creates the culture, which produces commitment, which produces performance from highly motivated staff. A good leader will be able to read the mood and motivation of their staff, and adapt their style accordingly.

> **In challenging times, it's the leaders with a "can-do" attitude, those who are confident and who are attentive to the concerns of their people, who will succeed.**

In the real world, the scales often lean to the task/job/objectives side, and when the going gets tough, what we as leaders need are motivated staff who are committed to their work and are willing to put in that bit extra. But to get there, to work through until such a time that the scales level again, they must feel that there **will** be a time when their leader focuses more on the people than the job.

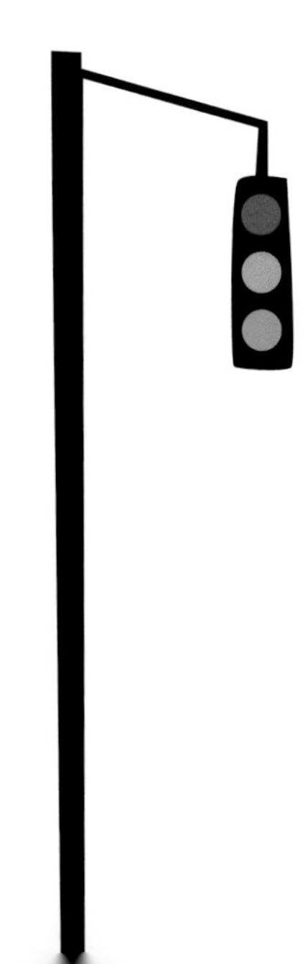

So what is a company's most important asset? Of course everybody says the people, but do they live it? The following chapters will suggest some hints and tips on how to lead this very important asset so that it is working at its best. For those of you who are more sceptical or finance-minded, you could look at it in terms of return on investment; the better the leadership culture, the better the return on investment.

> **What we should all want for our bus journey is to share the experience with people who share the same goal, live by the same standards, who actually want to be on the bus and, finally, who are motivated to do what is needed to reach the end of the journey, despite any obstacles along the way.**

KEY WORDS TO LEADERSHIP

PERSONAL
RESPONSIBILITY
COMMUNICATION
TEAMWORK
EMPOWERMENT
INNOVATION
MOTIVATION
LEAD BY EXAMPLE
DELEGATION
BEHAVIOURS
INCLUSION
CHALLENGE
CREATIVITY

LEADERSHIP TIPS FOR THE BUS

Before setting off
on your bus journey:

- Set clear objectives (if you have the opportunity, **include** your team in setting/agreeing these goals)
- Communicate the final objectives to **ALL** your team and in a language they understand
- Get **'buy in'** from your team – get them onboard your bus willingly
- Make sure your team members are aware of their 'fare' – what they need to contribute to the journey and how they will help to make the journey successful
- Equally, what they will gain from the journey and/or reaching their final destination
- When all are onboard, close the door and leave the station

During
the bus journey:

- Keep your entire team focused on the same goal so that personal needs become secondary to the needs of the team and the task
- Understand and use effectively - responsibility, authority & accountability
- The culture you aim to achieve is openness, honesty, personal responsibility, trust & support
- Encourage **regular, clear communication** throughout
- Give your team the opportunity to be creative
- Empower them to make decisions and challenge them to stretch their abilities
- Delegate tasks
- Lead by example

At the end
of the bus journey:

- Success breeds success
  – so celebrate the win

CHAPTER 2
COMMUNICATION

> "HEAR THE MEANING WITHIN THE WORD."
>
> WILLIAM SHAKESPEARE

Excellent communication is the foundation of effective leadership. But before we look at communication and leadership together, I think it would be valuable to first look at communication in its own right.

That's because without communication we can't do anything worthwhile that involves other people. In fact, the ability to communicate across time as well as space has been described as one of the traits that defines us as humans. Communication is such an important and central part of our lives that if we think of it at all it is usually because something has gone wrong. And maybe that's the problem; we don't think about it enough.

> **Poor communication is at the root of just about every problem in the workplace.**

Sometimes our brains and our mouths don't quite work together. Someone misinterprets a word we use, and they take offence. We unconsciously talk down to someone, and they take offence. And, of course, ninety-nine times out of a hundred none was meant. But it's too late – the damage is done and communication has been severed, perhaps to the point that it ceases altogether. So why can this happen? Because we don't adhere to a logical process.

> **How different things would be if we all understood each other all the time!**

With just a little more thought on the part of the sender, greater understanding can be achieved for the receiver, and that makes a positive outcome much more likely. But this means the sender has to take responsibility for communication as well as take into account the inevitable barriers that crop up.

Let's take a look at the 5 steps of the communication process:

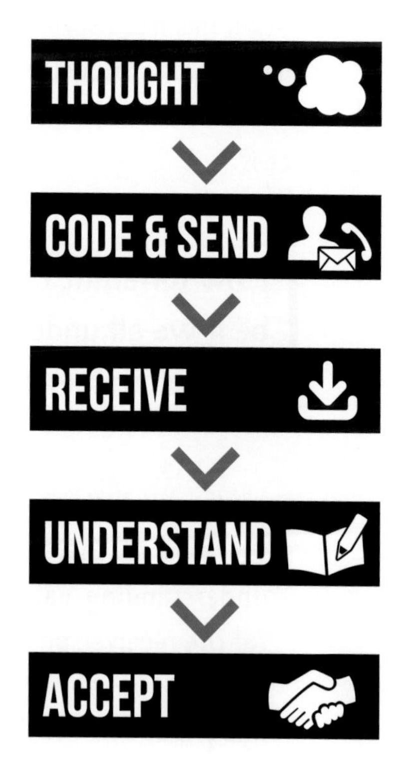

THOUGHT

Do you, the sender, fully understand what the objective(s) is (are) before communicating? Have you thought about who it needs to be sent to? What do you know about the receiver? Is the thought process in the correct order for the receiver? Does the receiver harbour any prejudice against you or the subject?

CODE & SEND

Is it coded correctly for the receiver? Should it be in email, telephone, verbal, or letter format? If the communication is meant for multiple receivers, is the one form of code effective for all?

RECEIVE

Have you checked it has actually been received?

UNDERSTAND

Has it really been understood? Has someone taken offence? Has it been misread or read into? Does the receiver understand all the words?

ACCEPT

Have you simply assumed the communication has been accepted?

The above are just a few examples of the potential barriers to communication, but I'm sure you can think of lots more. For me, this confirms just how easy it is for communication to go badly wrong and, therefore, how very important it is to follow the process through.

Here are **three** key things to remember that will make communication more effective:

EMPLOY FEEDBACK

If you can involve the other person, they'll invest more in understanding and accepting your message. But you'll need to do more than just invite questions; people will often just say no - perhaps through fear, or not wanting to embarrass themselves. Remember, you can still encourage the two-way process by asking questions yourself.

KNOW YOUR RECEIVER

The better you understand them, the easier it will be for you to communicate in a way that meets their needs and expectations. Think about the language they will understand - what they already know, and how they feel about both you and the subject.

PLAN

What will the receiver do upon hearing you? Think about how, where, and when you communicate. How will those things influence the receiver? What do they need to know in order to do (or not do!) what you want?

I'm sure that by now you can see why I think communication is of **paramount importance** when you talk about leadership. The good news is that communication is a skill like any other, and anyone can learn to be more effective in it. Any time invested can pay massive dividends, because the way in which we interact with each other can be the difference between success and failure when leading teams.

Communication is the foundation of leadership.

> " MEND YOUR SPEECH A LITTLE, LEST YOU MAY MAR YOUR FORTUNES. "
>
> WILLIAM SHAKESPEARE

Failure to communicate effectively wastes resources - not least as a result of rework. Consider the cost every time a member of your team misunderstands a request and does the wrong thing. They have to be asked again, leading to delay, the resource put into the original request was wasted, and this quite probably led to poor customer service. The role we play in any business is ultimately for the benefit of our customers and if we are less than effective it will always adversely affect them.

Remember, people are different and all have their own communication styles.

> **We as leaders should take responsibility to adapt our communication style to that of the team member we are communicating with.**

True leaders create a culture of inclusion, empowerment, and trust – a fully cohesive team - and this can only happen if communication is a two way process.

We want creativity, we want to know when things are going wrong before it's too late to put them right and we want our staff to feel that they can communicate with us whatever the issue. How can we achieve this?

ASK QUESTIONS

Asking the right questions is not easy; how and when a question is asked is as important as the motive behind its asking.

Skilfully done, we can encourage people to express doubts, fears, and objections, as well as provide us with information. The key to good questioning lies in understanding the three dimensions of any question: is it open or closed, is it general or specific, is it neutral or laden?

Open questions can't be answered simply with facts. These are the questions to which the length and nature of the answer depends upon the other person - we invite them to freely express their thoughts, feelings and opinions. For example, you might learn a great deal by asking "What is it about our solution that bothers you?" But the best invitations needn't even be questions at all – you might say "tell me...", or "explain how...", or "describe what...".

> **Open questions encourage people to talk to you, and show that you are interested in what they have to say.**

Closed questions automatically limit the answer to a "yes, no, black, white" response. Generally, they are far less valuable unless you want strictly factual information – a specific point such as a name or date (although they can be useful for politely shutting down a talkative person).

> **Ask them a closed question about their point, and then ask an open one about yours!**

Closed questions are always specific, but an open question may be general or specific. A general question is often a good way to open up a topic for discussion, following up with more specific ones to obtain more detail. A typical sequence of questions might run like this:

- Tell me about your present role
- Which aspects of the role did you enjoy most?
- Why did you feel that way about that particular task?
- How often did you have to carry out that task?
- Did you work on this task alone?

These questions are successively more focussed, with the last one representing a closed, and therefore specific, question.

What I've said here isn't, of course, absolute. You might really **need** to ask a question that's closed and thoroughly loaded with value judgements, but the best way to find out what people really think is to use open, neutral questions that encourage them to talk. More specific – even closed - questions can always be used later to narrow things down. But perhaps even more important than using the correct questions is the need to create a friendly, encouraging atmosphere in which people decide to communicate of their own volition - **leadership at its best!**

> “Asking the right questions takes as much skill as giving the right answers.”
>
> Robert Half

Remember, however, that we haven’t finished with a question once it has been asked – we need to listen carefully to the reply and interpret its meaning. Depending on the results of this process, which we often have to manage on the run, our follow-up questions may need to be modified.

LISTENING

Some research suggests that the average leader spends at least 40% of their day "listening". It's fundamental to most jobs, because most jobs involve communication with other people, and effective decision making requires us to obtain and analyse the information we hear, as well as that which we see.

> **Day-to-day relationships with our team and colleagues all depend on the ability to listen effectively.**

Hearing is passive, listening is active.

But even when we are really listening, we don't always do so at the same level.

Consider the following:

LEVEL 1 - involves the distinguishing of words – simply making sense out of the sounds we hear. It's more a general "awareness", an ambient noise.

LEVEL 2 - we begin to understand. We concentrate on what is being said, and the differences between words and their meanings become significant.

LEVEL 3 - involves us in distinguishing fact from fiction, truth from lies, and so requires of us some degree of analysis.

LEVEL 4 - is that which requires the greatest degree of skill and concentration, and involves the added dimension of empathy: we seek to understand what is being said from the **speaker's** point of view.

> “You cannot truly listen to anyone, and do anything else at the same time.”
>
> M. Scott Peck

So how do we become better listeners? The above steps are simple enough – we just have to remember to apply them, especially when we are under pressure. But how can we increase our ability to listen as we should?

Follow the three key points below:

PREPARATION

Plan to eliminate distractions (noise, views, people, etc.) and concentrate on your speaker. Always give yourself enough time to listen and be ready to respond, but not too hastily.

ATTITUDE

Find an area of interest in what is being said. If your aim is to receive ideas, you need an objective to focus on. However, stay flexible enough to change your aim if necessary. Try to judge the content of a message rather than the person sending it.

> **Good listeners keep an open mind about the speaker and the subject, and put their prejudices to one side.**

Only evaluate when you have thoroughly understood. Concentrate on the meaning of what is said and the feelings behind it, not just the words themselves. Give yourself time to mentally summarise what you have heard, but be careful not to switch into "think mode" for too long and miss the speaker's next words.

DEMONSTRATION

Let the speaker know you're listening and provide encouragement. An alert posture, eye contact, encouraging words, a question - even a smile - will all show that you are listening.

In simple terms, the more effective a communicator you become, the better your leadership skills. It takes hard work and practise, and for most of us it does not come naturally. Use the 5 stage process, question effectively, and listen with empathy.

You will gain a skill that will not only make you a more effective leader, but will also show that you are inclusive, that you care about your team, and that you are interested in their ideas and thoughts.

> “THE EAR OF THE LEADER MUST RING WITH THE VOICES OF THE PEOPLE.”
>
> WOODROW WILSON

KEY WORDS TO COMMUNICATION

PLAN
QUESTION
EMPATHY
FEEDBACK
TWO-WAY
LISTEN
BARRIERS
SUMMARISE
CODE
CLARITY
ATTITUDE
CHECK

COMMUNICATION TIPS FOR THE BUS

Before, during and after

the bus journey:

- Plan your communication - **always use the process shown** – it doesn't have to take long
- Know your receiver – they are your passengers, get to know them
- Think of the receiver's communication style
  - Use theirs not yours **(it is you that needs to change your approach)**
- Think about the code that you intend to use (e.g. email, telephone, etc.)
- You may need to use more than one code
  - One code may not suit multiple audiences
- Think of what the barriers could be – then try to overcome them

- Ask questions
- Listen to the answers
- Check understanding – don't assume
- Summarise – ensure both parties understand the communication
- Don't leave things unsaid
- Know when you have said enough and move on
- Consider body language – more in the next chapter
- Seek feedback – find out what your receiver really thinks and feels

At any stage of the bus journey you should be asking and checking to see if your communication style is appropriate for what is required. If not, what are **you** going to do about it?

> **Remember, ineffective or a lack of communication are the most common complaints from team members.**

CHAPTER 3

NON-VERBAL COMMUNICATION

> "THE MOST IMPORTANT THING IN COMMUNICATION IS HEARING WHAT ISN'T SAID."
>
> PETER F. DRUCKER

Non-verbal communication, or NVC, is the final piece of the jigsaw when becoming a really effective communicator. In fact, **NVC forms the bulk of our communication**, which is why the subject has a chapter all to itself.

However, before we look at the role of NVC in effective leadership, we need to look at it in general terms if we are to first understand why it's so important and why we ignore it at our peril. First of all, NVC is the main channel for communicating emotion which, in turn, is a powerful driver of behaviour. This affects how people perceive and understand each other, so in order to be a fully effective communicator, you must be able to understand and interpret NVC.

We base our emotional responses to another person not so much upon what they say, but upon how they say it, how they look, and how they behave. NVC is not just about body language, but covers anything implicit in our interactions other than actual words. Only a small portion of the message in any communication comes from your choice of words. In fact, research in the late 1960s shows that in a face-to-face situation:

- 7% comes from verbal communication (the words you use)
- 38% is based on the ways in which the words were said - tone of voice, emphasis, etc.
- 55% depends on what is seen - facial expressions, posture, gestures, and so forth

This means that **over 90% of a given message is conveyed through NVC** and that it can either support what you say, or contradict it. If what people see contradicts what you say they will almost invariably choose to believe their eyes, which can have a huge impact on your ability to communicate effectively. For the sceptics, even if we allow for 20% inaccuracy, 70% of what we communicate face-to-face is based on something other than the words we use. I like to think that you all share key information with your staff and would hope that most of that sharing is done face-to-face. If this is the case, I'm sure that you fully understand why this subject is so important and one to learn more about.

To be clear, please don't think that NVC doesn't matter on the telephone or in writing, because it does. Of course, on the telephone there is no visual component, but NVC still has a huge impact. 80% of the message is now conveyed by how you say the words (tone, pitch, volume etc.) and, though the impact of the words has increased, they still only convey 20% of the message. In writing meanwhile, the words carry a much greater part of the load, but their tone and formality, as well as aspects like emphasis, formatting and style, will still have a considerable effect on how people perceive the writer and their message.

Fortunately, reading and understanding NVC is a skill like any other, one that you can learn through practice, experience and feedback. The more effective you are at using these skills, the more effective you will become as a communicator – an essential characteristic of a leader. As you review the rest of this chapter, just remember the benefits:

- Good NVC from you supports and reinforces your words, instead of contradicting them
- You can use NVC to establish the right conditions for your message to be accepted
- Being able to read NVC will give you valuable feedback on how the receiver is reacting to your message

There are many different aspects to NVC and the better you understand them, the more you can use them to:

- Understand and judge what people are telling you (or what they are not, as the case may be)
- Have more input as to how they feel about the information you are sharing
- Read their level of interest, passion, commitment and so forth
- Get a feel for attitude, sense of personal responsibility and motivation

So let's break NVC down a little more into two key areas - paralinguistics and body language.

PARALINGUISTICS

Really, this is a long word used to describe the study of how things are said - **the NVC we hear, rather than see.** It covers quite a wide range of things, particularly tone of voice, which is one of the key ways in which emotions and feelings are revealed. Think of how your tone of voice changes when you are angry, sad, confident, nervous, or happy. Your words may not change, but the way in which you say them certainly will. Here are some examples of paralinguistic signals:

Speed of delivery – useful in support of other indicators. Hurried speech could indicate nervousness or just lack of time, whereas calm, measured speech may indicate confidence.

Pitch – a high pitch could indicate emotional stress, fear, or even anger.

Volume – a loud voice may be an indicator of stress or anger, or perhaps just excitement or passion.

Emphasis – accents on particular syllables or words can be important indicators of one's underlying feelings about the subject.

Silence – what isn't said is often as important as what is said. If you ignore or fill that silence, you may miss a really important underlying aspect.

> “WHEN THE EYES SAY ONE THING, AND THE TONGUE ANOTHER, A PRACTICED MAN RELIES ON THE LANGUAGE OF THE FIRST.”
>
> RALPH WALDO EMERSON

BODY LANGUAGE

This is the NVC we see rather than hear - words may lie, but the body rarely does. Some of the signals are common to all human beings (we're born with them), but we also pick up signals learned from our cultural environment that are very hard to unlearn. Either way, what matters is that many of the signals sent out by your body happen subconsciously as the brain reacts and sends automatic instructions to your face, limbs, and other parts of the body.

Things like:

Bodily Contact, Proximity, Orientation – how close we stand to others, where we sit, orientation of physical devices such as desks and chairs, all of which can enhance one's status.

Appearance – the clothes we wear, hairstyles, grooming, jewellery - all give unspoken messages about us that the receiver interprets. For example, you wouldn't (unless by prior arrangement) go to an important client meeting in old jeans and a t-shirt because you would probably be classed as unprofessional, and the client may think that reflects the way in which you work.

Gestures – a clenched fist, a pointed finger, or steepled hands, which are usually a sign of self-confidence or even dominance. For instance, a shuffling of chairs or the rustling of papers can indicate a meeting has gone on for too long.

Head Movements – a raised head may indicate interest, openness, or control of a situation. Alternatively, a lowered head may indicate doubt, dissatisfaction, defeat, or insecurity.

Posture & Stance – individual gestures are more meaningful when linked to other aspects of the body's posture. For example, a forward posture with a smile may indicate warmth and encouragement. Without a smile, it may indicate determination or even a desire to dominate. Raised shoulders indicate tension, whereas lowered shoulders mean someone is more relaxed.

Facial Expressions – these are more commonly controlled than many other aspects of body language. We probably all know someone with a poker face, so be aware that facial expressions may not always be a true reflection of thought or attitude. Various combinations are possible and, along with signals from the eyes, can indicate a huge range of feelings - happy, sad, perplexed, intrigued, worried, angry, sceptical, bored, and so forth.

Eye Contact – we make eye contact when we like the other person or we are interested in what they are saying. If someone is not making eye contact with you, then you want to be looking for other signals to ensure that you are interpreting their NVC correctly. As an example, they may be under-confident, feel threatened or uninterested.

The better you know and understand how someone reacts to changing circumstances, the more you will understand what might be going on in their head. Here is a simple example: If you want to win at poker, skill with the cards and a bit of luck are obviously important. Just as essential, however, is an ability to work out how good or bad other people's cards might be, all the while making sure that they can't do the same to you. **It's almost impossible for someone to truly hide how they feel,** so you listen carefully to what they say, but judge whether or not they are bluffing by their NVC. The way they sit, a little smile or grimace, whether they talk more or less, all can tell you something.

> THE BODY NEVER LIES.
>
> MARTHA GRAHAM

Always bear in mind that **it is easy to misinterpret a stand-alone signal** - one 'signal' on its own is not enough to make a solid judgement. You need to read the NVC picture as a whole. A reliable assessment typically needs 3 signals all pointing in the same direction, usually described as a **'cluster'**.

For example, someone with a loud booming voice may just be hard of hearing, but a loud booming voice, a frown, a pointing finger and standing way too close suggest aggression when seen together. **It takes practice and you do have to be careful.** We also have to allow for cultural differences, because behavioural indicators can mean different things in different locations.

Reading clustered paralinguistic and body language signals as you communicate with your team will help you to understand their true attitude, 'buy in', and feelings, both individually and collectively. The more open and honest your culture, the easier it will be to read the NVC of your team and other colleagues. In other circumstances, however, you may need to work harder to be able to interpret NVC effectively.

Don't forget that **your own NVC needs to support your message:** if you look and sound confident in yourself and your message, people will tend to believe that you are – even if you really feel otherwise. A leader always needs to at least sound and look as if they know what they're doing if they really want their team to follow them and stay on that bus!

I've only scratched the surface of this subject, but I hope to have shown you **how important NVC is to effective communication and, therefore, to leadership.**

KEY WORDS TO NON-VERBAL COMMUNICATION

FACIAL EXPRESSIONS
GESTURES
PITCH
EMPHASIS
TONE
EYE CONTACT
APPEARANCE
PROXIMITY
SPEED
POSTURE
SILENCE
CLUSTERS

NON-VERBAL COMMUNICATION TIPS FOR THE BUS

- Listen with your eyes and your ears - your passengers may have underlying feelings or emotions that they find difficult to convey to you
- Read your passenger's body language to sense their feelings and attitudes
- Make sure your own body language says "I'm here to help you"
- Use appropriate gestures to reinforce your spoken message
- Make eye contact with your passengers
- Encourage your passengers to read and interpret NVC

- Don't base a judgement on one signal alone - look for clusters
- Listen to your passenger's change in tone of voice, pitch, and so forth
- Seek feedback – ask your passengers in an encouraging manner if you 'feel' an underlying issue has not been brought to light
- Never go for the jugular – be careful and check that your NVC signals are giving you the correct message

CHAPTER 4
MOTIVATION

> "THE ONLY WAY OF FINDING THE LIMITS OF THE POSSIBLE IS BY GOING BEYOND THEM INTO THE IMPOSSIBLE."
>
> ARTHUR C. CLARKE

I often find it strange that when I ask the delegates on my workshops about the importance of motivation, the answer isn't always 'very'. Wouldn't you want to be on bus full of people that chose to be there rather than feel they have to be? Motivation is all about wanting to do something, and if we **want** to do something we do it **more efficiently, effectively and accurately.**

Looking at it another way, **every person who works for us is a volunteer** - they decide whether to take the job in the first place, and they can decide to quit at any time. Of course, we might have the power to fire them if they don't perform, and that **might** motivate them **if** they are afraid of being sacked! But do you want people on your bus that are driven by fear? I hope not - they will only do just enough to avoid the consequences. This is not what I call motivation. Working in a culture of fear means that initiative, creativity, anything that might get them into trouble, goes out the window. In place of that comes resentment - the "us versus them" mentality where management is concerned.

Surely what we want is for our people to identify with our objectives – **to actively want to do their very best.** Achieving this mentality is what motivation is all about. However, it is easy to get it wrong. Just think about how many people start a new job full of enthusiasm, high expectation and commitment. Then think how often that initial motivation quickly descends into routine, boredom - the same old stuff. How that happens and what we can do to prevent it is the million dollar question. The answer surely starts with what people get from their work.

> "Knowing is not enough;
> we must apply
> Willing is not enough;
> we must do."
>
> Johann Wolfgang von Goethe

We all work for lots of different reasons. The first priority for most people is to satisfy their basic needs: food, shelter, clothing, education for the kids, and so on. Of course we are often lucky enough in our society that we mostly have those covered. So what we in fact need from our job is our lifestyle. For many people, the necessities are all they get from their job and they may instead look for their higher needs elsewhere – perhaps through volunteer work, or family, or in a hobby or sport. In that difference lies the key.

If you want your people to be motivated, it's not enough to simply provide them with the necessities. The experts all agree that things like pay, work environment, terms and conditions, and skilled supervision are only the foundations. If you get these wrong, your staff will be de-motivated, but nothing you do in these areas will motivate them to do more than is required. To really get them onboard the bus (and stay on it) you need to delve much deeper.

So how can we find out what motivates our people? The simple answer is to ask them. People are motivated by different things and making assumptions is not good enough. In fact, many of the people you ask won't have actually thought about it themselves. If they don't know what motivates them, how are you supposed to?

Why not try it yourself and take a second or two to think about what motivates you? It is possible that the same applies to you, and if you don't know how is your line manager going to motivate you?

Have a look at the few I've listed here:

> **Job satisfaction, personal growth & development, promotion, a sense of achievement, feeling valued, recognition, a sense of belonging, working in a happy environment, the people you work with, challenge, work/life balance, empowerment.**

This is not an exhaustive list by any means, but may help you if you are trying to explain to your team what you are talking about when you mention the word motivation.

If you have more than one person in your team, each may be motivated by different things, an important factor to remember if you want a high-performing team on your bus.

When I'm working with individuals on this subject, I ask them to look at the motivation curve drawn as a diagram below. You'll see there are three numbers on the curve which indicate different possible behavioural cycles individuals can go through. Let's look at the typical behaviours that are shown in each cycle:

MOTIVATION CURVE

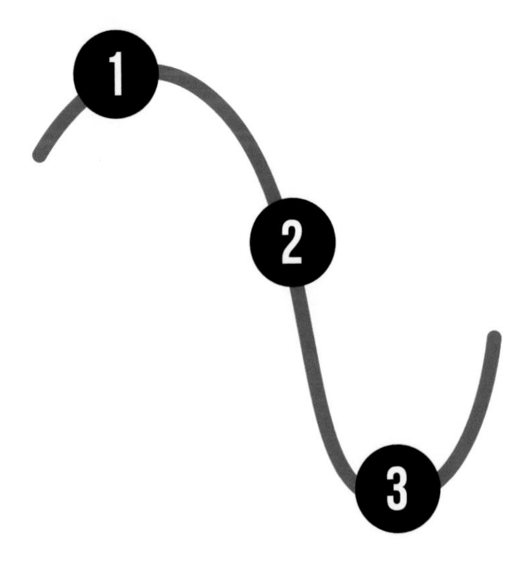

1.

Those that are motivated! We spend less time with this group because we think that they are fine and doing a great job (in fact, they exceed expectations). Typically, **they are enthusiastic, positive, happy, helpful, supportive, driven, creative, confident, honest, willing and pro-active individuals.** The problem here, however, is if we don't find out what keeps them motivated they may start sliding down the curve. Before we know it, they are a swinger (2).

3.

Those that are de-motivated! These people are already at the bottom of the curve and are the ones we spend most of our time with. Typical behaviours can include **boredom or cynicism. They can also be disruptive, ineffective, frustrated, stressed, emotional, depressed, angry or just plain negative individuals with matching behaviours.** These people may have been 1s, but for whatever reason (which we missed) they have hit rock bottom. They could be ready to leave, and they will definitely be affecting other team members, possibly by dragging them down too. Alternatively, they may just spend their time complaining about how bad things are. These are not the people you want on your bus, and can be very difficult to re-motivate.

2.

Those I call **'swingers'!** These people are either on the way down to 3, or on the way up to 1. If they are on their way down, and haven't gone too far, you have a real chance of finding out what the issues are and of getting them back onboard. If they get all the way to a 3, it is much more difficult to really get them back onboard and wholly re-motivated. This is not impossible, however, and it is important to not give up at the first attempt. Spending all your time on these individuals, however, means you may well be missing the **1s** just starting on that downward spiral, so be aware.

The key thing to take from this chapter is to take the time to understand what makes your people tick, no matter how busy you may be. It's not about the money – it's about how they feel about the job. Why? Because this is a virtuous circle -

> **the better motivated people are, the more they achieve, and the more job satisfaction they experience, the more motivated they are!**

How would it feel if all your team **chose** to follow your lead with commitment and enthusiasm? That's the satisfaction (and motivation) that real leaders experience. As you continue through further chapters, you will see that motivation is a driver in many of them.

KEY WORDS TO MOTIVATION

EMPOWERMENT
QUESTION
PASSION
WILLING
ENTHUSIASM
SUPPORT
CHALLENGE
COMMUNICATION
BELIEF
ENCOURAGEMENT
PERSONAL RESPONSIBILITY
POSITIVITY

MOTIVATION TIPS FOR THE BUS

- **Make the time** to find out what motivates each and every passenger on the bus
- Build the right atmosphere - create an environment in which your passengers can thrive
- Give rewards when deserved - rewards don't always cost money
- Promote the worth of the job - the person that cleans the bus is as important as the driver
- Keep them informed - **the biggest complaint of many teams is the lack of communication**
- Be fair in allocation - make all your passengers feel valued, not one or two
- Allow for circumstances - without a doubt, your route will change or you may even have to stop without warning

- Avoid threats to security
- Clear targets and objectives – be clear with the passengers about expectations for both parties
- Offer training and personal development – keep the passengers' minds open and developing
- Feedback – give it and receive it on a daily basis
- **Make work fun – a happy bus is successful**

CHAPTER 5

TEAMWORK

> “Coming together is a beginning, staying together is progress, and working together is success.”
>
> Henry Ford

If your bus is to be successful, the passengers on it need to work as a team. Of course, this is a very simple concept, but it's not so easy to realise. Many groups of individuals believe that they are working as a team, but their actions and behaviours show something different.

I see this contradiction all the time, and more often than not the signs are very clear:

- Each individual thinks of their own needs first
- Others are blamed for failure, while success is claimed by the individual
- Information is power, so people don't share, and are not open and honest with their thoughts and feelings
- People push their own agenda at the expense of other team members, and value only one approach - theirs!

I could go on, but I hope these few examples show that these behaviours can never be those of a high-performing team. So, what might a real team look like?

- Every member thinks of the team first and themselves second
- Each takes full responsibility for their actions (no blame culture, see Chapter 10)
- Information is shared and communication is assertive and candid
- Team members are valued - they share common goals, values and loyalties

With these behaviours, individuals succeed when the team succeeds, and will see their own growth and development within that context, rather than by comparison to other team members. This allows individuals to think about the needs and wants of their colleagues, and encourages them to go out of their way to ensure the team achieves, even if they don't personally. Cultivating this environment is key to developing a positive collective mindset.

So, which approach would you like on your bus? A group of individuals may get to the end of the journey at some stage, but the high-performing team will arrive more quickly and efficiently. Perhaps more importantly, **they will also be a happier, more motivated team when they do reach their final destination.**

> "IF A TEAM IS TO REACH ITS POTENTIAL, EACH PLAYER MUST BE WILLING TO SUBORDINATE HIS PERSONAL GOALS TO THE GOOD OF THE TEAM."
>
> BUD WILKINSON

As line managers, yet another role is to regularly review our team. We must ensure that the dynamics are healthy, that the behaviours and actions of individuals and the team are appropriate, and that our team continues to grow and develop. We must lead by example in all of these areas, and provide empowerment, autonomy and challenges to support them.

To move forward, we need to look at team dynamics, standards, and the behaviours and attitudes required of a high-performing team.

Below, I've identified 5 key areas that you need to tick off before you can call your group of individuals a team:

- A shared goal or purpose
- All working together to produce the end result
- Common standards shared by all, and the discipline to stick to them
- Cohesion and co-operation
- An open and honest culture

If any one of these is missing, it's just not a team. A sales "team" working on commission, for example, may tick four of these, but they may not really be working together if they ultimately compete for sales!

> "INDIVIDUALS PLAY THE GAME, BUT TEAMS BEAT THE ODDS."
>
> SEAL TEAM SAYING

Like anything that is worthwhile, building a high-performing team takes time, commitment, belief from the leader, **and** belief from the individuals.

Let's consider how this can be achieved by first looking at the four stages that all teams go through when they form – and which surface again whenever the members of the team change. It doesn't matter if a team is forming for a few months or for a longer period, the process is the same. The only variable is that we may stay in a given stage for a much shorter period of time.

> **As leaders, our role is to guide the team through this process so that the outcome is positive at each stage - however difficult it may seem at the time.**

This is how the process goes:

FORMING

When a group of individuals meet for the first time the dynamic is generally very nice and polite. People are a little reserved and watchful – after all, they don't know each other. What's happening at this stage is that we are weighing each other up (even if we don't admit it). We want to see where they – and we – are going to fit in.

Humans make decisions about new people within the first 90 seconds of contact, and in the early stages of opinion formation we are subconsciously drawn to those who we think are like us – whether or not that eventually turns out to be true. At this stage we are setting the scene, working out our collective standards, establishing relationships and metering behaviours. The leader's job at this stage is to build the value of each team member and open up channels of communication before you all go off and start working together.

STORMING

As people get to know each other better, they start trying to establish their rightful place in the team. For some, this will mean jockeying for position, testing each other out, challenging each other (and you), and essentially questioning the status quo. People will react to this in different ways, and this can (and probably will) lead to some conflict and confrontation.

> **Leaders and teams often try to dodge this stage because it's uncomfortable, even challenging, but this stage is vital to building the team and is going to happen anyway.**

The good news, however, is that if we can keep the storming focused on the task, and make sure that behaviours and communication are open, constructive, and assertive, this stage is also a great opportunity. It allows us to see the strengths and weaknesses of each team member, to encourage them to support and learn from each other, and to establish the foundation for team norms. As a leader, our job is to build an open, honest forum in which the **entire** team feels free to voice their issues without any comeback or negativity. Small grievances or issues can be raised and dealt with promptly before they get out of hand, and we can avoid the bickering and divisive cliques which so badly affect the dynamics and culture of the team.

NORMING

A strong culture grows out of common purpose and common standards, and those elements grow out of the storming stage. If you have guided that stage effectively then team norms will be positive and you can get on with the everyday business of the team in an effective, cohesive manner. The team will be in a comfortable place and contain members who are considerate of each other, are secure and empowered, and working together efficiently and effectively. Team members will continue to build on their relationships in an open and honest fashion, roles will be clear, issues will be addressed, and they will support each other in achieving the overall team goals rather than just their own. Indeed, team norms are so important to effective team-work that I'm going to come back to them later in this chapter.

PERFORMING

So what makes the difference between an OK team and an excellent one? Both are built on these same foundations, but the very best teams are energised by high levels of challenge, energy, pace and support, a strong goal focus, a positive mindset and very definitely high levels of candour and morale.

> **What's more, when the going gets tough, everyone pulls together and gives their all, even at a cost to themselves.**

To achieve this, team members must be empowered, trusted, and given opportunities to grow, develop, and be creative. There is no blame culture; team members follow the team standards willingly, are motivated, and want to be the best. I would certainly want this team on my bus, but I believe this can only be achieved when you as a leader lead by example. Leaders need to exhibit the behaviours and attitudes we explored in Chapter 1, and encourage everyone else to do the same. If team members are not living the team norms, then it is your responsibility to pick it up immediately before it causes problems and harms the team's cohesion. To put it simply – **that which you permit, you promote.**

CLARITY OF EXPECTATION

I keep referring to team standards or norms, so let's see what I mean. First off, I would define team standards as an agreed set of actions or behaviours that all team members agree to follow. Below, I've broken them down into six categories:

Work — The easiest and most efficient criteria for working, including speed, duration, standard and depth.

Attitudes — The beliefs and values underpinning the attitudes that drive the culture of the team.

Behaviours — Topics that can be discussed and those that cannot, the behaviours considered acceptable, and those that are not.

Clothes	The team uniform standards and modes of dress in various scenarios.
Language	Forms of language considered acceptable, again in various scenarios: slang, technical terms, nicknames, jokes, etc.
Morals	Permissible levels of time-wasting, scrounging, truth-telling, sexual behaviour, etc.

Company policy usually takes care of the big stuff, but team norms often cover areas which have much more impact on the subjective performance of a given team. Of course, sometimes they can seem quite trivial in themselves – that is, until they go wrong! It is for the leader, during the forming stage, to make sure that those norms established by the team are acceptable and appropriate.

Having standards that everybody accepts also means that if anyone (including the boss...) gets something wrong, another member of the team can pull them up without fear of a poor reaction. Clarity of expectation supports a culture of personal responsibility and open communication within a team that enjoys the characteristics mentioned earlier. Before you consider what your team standards are, however, there are some key questions to ask:

- Do you already have some agreed standards? If not, what should they be? If so, what works and what doesn't?

- Does everyone adhere to them? If not, why not?

- How are you going to make them work for your team?

Please remember, it is easier to set work standards, but don't forget that **we also need standards around behaviour** – these are key to a high-performing team. **Personal responsibility and positive thinking** in particular are two specific areas which directly affect our attitudes to team behaviour. These are discussed later in the book in Chapters 11 and 12 respectively. Also, please review Chapter 13 on feedback, because this will help you to support, guide, and deal with these issues. Feedback is also a great tool to help motivate your team members.

Finally, I believe that the following statement is an absolute truth inherent in all high-performing teams, and one that I want to reiterate in this context:

Teams and leadership are about 'we', not 'I'.

It may sound simple, but believe me it took me a long while to learn that lesson. I only wish that I had learned it earlier in my career. Being part of a high-performing team is rewarding; firstly, in contributing to the success of something bigger than ourselves, and secondly, in how much more you can personally grow and develop within a successful team.

So what's the outcome of all your hard work and commitment to building that team culture? When your bus reaches its destination (whatever the challenges you have faced and no doubt there will be plenty) you will still have a **motivated, positive, and committed team that is ready for the next journey.** Just remember to **celebrate** your success, allow a little downtime for the bus to be serviced, and for the passengers to get off and stretch their legs before setting off on your next adventure.

KEY WORDS TO TEAMWORK

COMMON GOALS
COOPERATION
MOTIVATION
PERSONAL RESPONSIBILITY
STANDARDS
HONESTY
SUPPORT
DISCIPLINE
ATTITUDE
COHESION
INCLUSION
CHALLENGE
OPENNESS

TEAMWORK TIPS FOR THE BUS

- Think team not 'I' – that goes for the passengers too
- Team culture doesn't happen on its own – you, the leader, have to develop it and encourage others to live it
- Be inclusive - don't leave your team behind – keep them on the bus with you
- Remember the 4 stage process – don't try to miss any steps
- Return to the 4 stage process every time you gain a new passenger
- Ensure you have team standards that work

- Don't let the standards set themselves – stop the bus and agree what they are with the passengers
- All team members have the same requirement to live by those standards set – whatever the role or position
- Remember, behaviours are a key aspect to teams and leadership – lead by example
- Don't let molehills grow into mountains – pick up the little issues or gripes as early as possible

CHAPTER 6
ASSERTIVENESS

> "THE BASIC DIFFERENCE BETWEEN BEING ASSERTIVE AND BEING AGGRESSIVE IS HOW OUR WORDS AND BEHAVIOUR AFFECT THE RIGHTS AND WELLBEING OF OTHERS."
>
> SHARON ANTHONY BOWER

Assertiveness means standing up for yourself but not at the expense of others or, to put it another way, asserting your rights while respecting theirs.

> **As leaders, we should always aim for assertive behaviours when dealing with our team members, and we should expect the same from them.**

You may wonder why I am stating the obvious, but while most people understand that assertive behaviour is desirable, even with the best will in the world, our behaviour often changes in response to the situation.

This happens particularly in difficult or challenging circumstances, times when we are under pressure and don't have the luxury to think about and plan our responses. In those situations an instinctive response often leads to less effective behaviour. So let's have a look at what can happen, why, and the impact those behaviours can have on the team, and on you as the leader.

As you can see from the diagram below, I believe assertiveness sits in the middle of a line between two other behaviours - passive at one end, and aggressive at the other. Assertiveness sits in a circle that covers a bigger chunk of the line, because we can all lean a bit one way or the other, sometimes without being seen as overly aggressive or overly passive. Real people are hardly ever bang in the middle, and nobody has much of a problem with this unless their behaviour goes too far one way or the other. Let's have a look at those behaviours and the problems that can crop up.

Passive behaviour is based on the underlying belief that other people's needs, views, feelings, ideas and beliefs are more important than our own. Consequently, people who behave passively tend not to express themselves openly, because they respect the rights of others so strongly that they put their own on the back-burner. They tend to **comply with the wants and needs of others while suppressing their own.** There are a number of reasons why people tend to lean towards passive behaviour, such as the need to be liked, to avoid conflict, the desire to please others, and – for some - just a sheer lack of confidence in themselves. All of this is fine if it is a deliberate choice – after all, you might willingly go with the flow to build a relationship, or because someone else knows better - but people who are overly passive tend to say 'yes' to things when they know they should really be saying 'no'.

This can cause them to feel like a victim, that they are being put upon, or forced to do things – all of which really means that they are not taking personal responsibility for their choices, and are blaming someone else for the situation (more on personal responsibility in Chapter 10).

> Passive people who agree to take on more than they can deliver clearly have time management issues, and often confuse passiveness with helpfulness and politeness.

In the short term, others may feel sorry for the passive person. They may feel sorry that they find situations difficult to handle, sorry that they don't speak up for themselves, they may even feel guilty for taking advantage of them. But after a while people tend to lose patience and respect for them. As work doesn't get completed, they become tired of being let down or of hearing these people moan and complain. Soon enough, **the morale and cohesion of the team is damaged.**

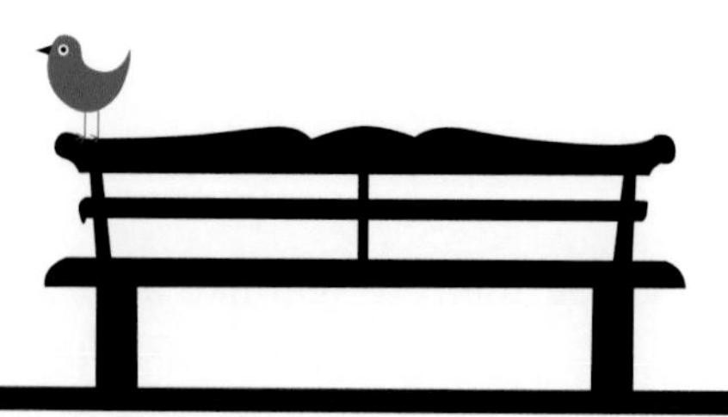

At the other end of the scale, we have **aggressive** behaviour. People behaving aggressively push for what they want, and are perfectly happy to ride roughshod over anyone who gets in their way. In other words, they have no respect for the rights of others. Generally, this means that **they believe their contribution to life and work is much more useful and important than anyone else's.** Overly aggressive people also tend to be focused to the point of being blinkered, to be dismissive of other people's opinions, to be loud, abrupt, and often direct to the point of rudeness. For them, it's "my way or the highway, and you'd better keep up". Watch out though, some aggressive behaviour is very open while some may be hidden and manipulative, but just as aggressive.

In the short term, aggressive people are often admired for their drive, focus, commitment, and for being forthright. However, it doesn't take long for those on the receiving end to feel angry, hurt, humiliated and resentful - feelings that make them want to retaliate. Aggression breeds aggression, openly or otherwise, and in the longer term, people working in a hostile environment will either leave, suffer miserably, or spend time plotting their revenge. In any case, **the work and the team will suffer.**

You wouldn't need too much of either behaviour on your bus for a new culture to start to develop, one of negativity, blame, lack of openness and honesty, and which will eventually lead to an underperforming team.

> “As we look ahead into the next century, leaders will be those who empower others.”
>
> Bill Gates

To avoid that negative culture, **leaders need to develop assertive behaviour in all members of the team.** The foundation for assertiveness is that everyone, whatever their role or position, believes that they have rights – especially the right to assert themselves – and that other people have the same. If this belief can be embedded and supported by action, then passive people will come to understand that being a doormat is no longer an effective or appropriate option, and aggressive people will learn that trampling over others is not either.

> **Assertive people are always looking for a win-win situation, to get what they want in collaboration with others, rather than at their expense.**

This breeds trust, confidence and mutual respect, a must if that bus is going to reach its destination intact and with a team of motivated people. It encourages the passive to come out of their shell and contribute, and lets the aggressive know that they can't always have their own way.

Now, I said that belief must be supported by action, and so **the leader needs to lead by example.** Now that we understand the passive, aggressive, and assertive in team members, let's look at this the other way round. How do team members see a leader who behaves in each of these ways?

PASSIVE

For a start, who's in charge? A passive leader can be wrapped around your little finger, but how can you respect that? Of course, they can get you to do their work for them, because **they are in control.** However, when the going finally gets tough you'll be on your own, unless you play the victim well enough and they take pity on you. If you show no self-belief, however, your team is unlikely to have confidence in you. They won't believe that you will stand up for them in tough times, or take responsibility with senior management when things go wrong. As a result, they'll hide things from you, and if you catch them out then they will still think they are right in their assertions. Being passive, you'll probably believe them.

AGGRESSIVE

On the other hand, if your team knows it's all about you they will be driven only by **fear** of consequence. This means they won't feel able to approach you with ideas or issues and will hide problems from you because they know that if anything goes wrong you'll hang them out to dry. Fear and respect are mutually exclusive. They won't respect you (not least because you don't respect them), so they will only communicate when they really have to. Forget initiative and creativity in this sort of environment; **people will do just enough to avoid your attention,** and will be delighted if you slip up and can't dodge the blame!

ASSERTIVE

If the team experiences assertive behaviour, however, they will feel respected, valued, and that you are on their side while still being the boss. In that environment, they feel able to approach you with suggestions and problems, that you want to help and support them, and that they can trust you. They'll believe that you will escalate issues appropriately, that you will stand up for them individually and as a team, and that you value their opinions. Trust is the basis of respect. Your team will listen to what you have to say and they will value your positive approach. When the going gets tough, **they will be right behind you, going out of their way to ensure success** because they **choose** to support you.

So, what type of leader would you like to be? Without a doubt, the only acceptable answer is assertive. As I mentioned at the beginning, with the best will in the world we all have days when our behaviour slips without us realising. In an open, supportive (and assertive) team, however, you'll soon get feedback when you get it wrong. If you're not sure about your own behaviour generally, the only way you can really find out is to seek feedback from your team and find out what they really think (for guidelines on feedback, see Chapter 13). It's a tough and scary thing to do, but **the perception of others is more important to leadership behaviours than what the leader thinks.**

I can relate to this because for years I thought that I was being assertive when I was really seen as aggressive. With the benefit of lots of hindsight and feedback I realised that, in fact, everyone else was right. It's a long time ago now, but if I didn't get my own way then I lived many of the behaviours you'll have noticed. Even though I achieved, it was not as much as I could have, and at the expense of good leadership. So how did I change? I took some simple (if occasionally tough) steps, which apply to both passive and aggressive people. I:

- Worked hard to be much more **self-aware**
- Identified the **triggers** that changed my behaviour
- Sought **feedback** from others

- Asked others for **help and support** – so that when I started to move towards aggressive behaviour, people told me before it became a problem
- Would review a situation and learn from my mistakes when I slipped by asking what I would do **differently** if the same circumstance happened again

It really works, and I know that because I still seek feedback. Of course, because I'm human, when my back's against the wall I can still slip into more aggressive behaviour. However, aggressive is no longer my default position, and all my team feel able to say "Whoa, Sue – you're off on one!" That's all I need to make me stop, think, and adapt my behaviour to take an assertive approach.

As leaders, we should set the example of openness to feedback so that we can continue to learn and develop ourselves.

Do you actively seek feedback on your behaviours from your staff? If not, **today** is the day to start. You will not know what they think about you and your leadership unless you ask them, and assertiveness is a good place to start (but please refer to Chapter 12 beforehand). Be warned, however; if you are on the passive side (or they are) then they may not want to be open for fear of upsetting you. Equally, if you sit at the aggressive end, they may just be too scared to tell you the truth.

Having reviewed your own behaviour, don't forget that it's part of your role to **review that of the other members of your team.** If you do have members of your team who are showing passive or aggressive behaviours, then you need to help them understand that those behaviours are not appropriate or effective (these should actually be part of your team standards, as discussed in Chapter 5). Then you need to support your team as they make any changes by helping them to see the downfalls, identify triggers, and generally raise their self-awareness. **Changing behaviour does not happen overnight,** but with commitment and continued feedback, new and more appropriate behaviours can become anyone's norm.

Finally, we come back to the type of behaviours that you want on your bus. I would hope that you prefer assertive behaviour, because this drives openness, equality, fairness, consistency, personal responsibility, support and so forth. That type of bus is more likely to arrive at its destination intact and ready for the next journey.

KEY WORDS TO ASSERTIVENESS

WIN-WIN
SELF-BELIEF
PERSONAL RESPONSIBILITY
CONFIDENCE
RIGHTS
FEEDBACK
SELF-AWARENESS
RESPECT
COURAGE
CO-OPERATION

ASSERTIVENESS TIPS FOR THE BUS

- **Lead by example** – show your passengers assertive behaviours
- Seek feedback from your passengers on your behaviours – and the people you regularly meet along the way
- Create a culture in which anything other than assertive behaviour is unacceptable
- Be open and honest with each other
- Help your passengers understand the benefits of assertive behaviour
- Offer your passengers the courage and support to try new ways of working if it is needed

- Help your passengers become more aware of their own behaviours – give them feedback
- Don't be afraid to pick up behavioural issues – if you don't pick them up, you're inadvertently saying that they are acceptable and other passengers will follow the examples set (see team standards, Chapter 5)

CHAPTER 7
TIME MANAGEMENT

> "LEADERSHIP IS THE ART OF GETTING SOMEONE ELSE TO DO SOMETHING YOU WANT DONE BECAUSE HE WANTS TO DO IT."
>
> DWIGHT D. EISENHOWER

Time management is a way of life. How you spend your time affects your mindset, your attitude, your behaviours, and your motivation. This, in turn, affects your habits and your results. Fundamentally, this means it affects the people around you – your team. As a line manager, your role is to set an example that your team wants to emulate. Your job is not only to manage your own time well, but also that of your team.

To put it into context, take a moment to think about how you feel at the end of the day when you haven't achieved what you expected - frustrated, de-motivated, negative - you may even find it hard to cope. Then think about how that affects your behaviour and your reactions to your team (and the other people in your life). How about a day during which you have achieved or even surpassed your expectations - feel good? Satisfied? Motivated? Positive, can do attitude? Which set of behaviours do you think gets the most out of your team?

Time management affects everyone around you.

Firstly, let's just look at you and your own time management.

Have you ever thought about what you would do if you had that extra hour a day people always wish for? An extra hour to finish that report that has been sitting on your desk for the last month, to spend quality time with your team, to leave work on time or even go to the gym? Maybe you could spend time with the kids or even sit down and have a bit of time to yourself. Unless your time management is already spot on, most of us can win some time back by following a few simple guidelines.

But first, let's try a little test.

Do you:

- put things off – "oh I'll do it tomorrow"?
- put things that, for some reason, you don't want to do to the bottom of the pile?
- have a chair at your desk inviting people to stop for a chat any time they choose?
- do all your urgent tasks first?
- check your email every time it pings?

If you answered **yes** more often than not, then I humbly suggest that you could manage your time more effectively. These are all **'time bandits'**, the things that steal your time without you knowing.

Most of us have what I call a 'wish list', a mental list of the things we want to achieve. Unfortunately, however, these wishes rarely become reality: we spend 80% of our time achieving 20% of what we want to achieve. This chapter is about living in the present rather than the future (or the past), but first you have to commit to making a change. Nothing will happen without a change in behaviour from you.

The key to time management is planning, prioritisation and discipline.

PLANNING

The first challenge is to fully understand what the goals are for you, your team, and the organisation. To do that, consider the following questions:

- What is my job - what am I here to achieve?
- What are my key objectives, and what must I do to progress them?
- What, therefore, are my priorities? What's urgent? What's important?

Write down the answers, turn them into objectives, make them measurable, and put them in order. Know what needs to be done so that you can evaluate how you are going to utilise your resources and those of your team, and the organisation, most effectively. The better you are at this planning stage, the more likely it is that your bus will reach its destination on time.

> **Objective setting is the foundation of effective time management.**

So let's look at what you can do to make this journey smoother – ways in which you can save the seconds to gain those minutes.

Consider how you actually spend your time. You are looking for the seepage. Obviously, it is easy to account for chunks of time in the day (meetings, writing a report etc.) but less so for the few hours that seem to vanish on a regular basis. The only way to **really** find out how you use your day is to keep an activity log. Keep a record of everything you do in a diary or on a piece of paper for a period of time - a week, or ideally a fortnight. Try to include everything, from the 10 minutes spent chatting to Jane, the 7 minutes helping Annie, the 5 minutes checking emails and then the 2 hour meeting. The more specific you can be, the more useful the information in the long term.

> **You cannot change something if you don't know what it is you need to change.**

After just a few days you should be able to identify with greater accuracy how frequently you engage in a certain activity and for how long. This also enables you to identify those items that do not contribute to your overall objectives. I have no doubt that with your line manager hat on you will also be in a position to identify those items that could be delegated to others with greater efficiency. This entails the identification of those **"high leverage"** activities - planning, training, delegation - that will repay an investment of your time in the long term.

Use the tools available to you. Use your diary to its fullest. Objectives can be split into 3 periods - long, medium and short term. What you do in the short term should help you to achieve the long term objectives.

Set **small** milestones along the way to ensure you enjoy small wins and can **check that you are on target.** Starting at the final desired outcome, work backwards and then book time out of your diary and your team's to ensure you have allocated enough time to achieve the objective. If this doesn't happen, more often than not the task gets put to one side until you are a couple of months down the road and it hasn't been started. Then you're forced into **reactive** rather than **proactive** mode.

There are things that you do every day, every month, every quarter. You know you have to do them (and should want to), but if they are not in your diary then they get pushed out or even ignored. If they are in your diary, however, and you do have to move them, then you are in a position to make a decision. Is what you are replacing them with more important? Will you move them to another time? Will you just cancel them? This allows you to make a considered judgement.

Put another way, when you book your annual holiday one of the first things you do is book time out of your diary. It is allocated time and something would need to be very important to move it. So should those quarterly meetings not carry the same weight as your holiday? Take a few minutes and think about the tasks you carry out regularly, how long they take, and whether you have booked sufficient time out of your diary to complete them. They are not going to go away, and if you don't book time out, when the time does come there will be no space left. As I have said, **planning and discipline are key!**

> EITHER RUN THE DAY OR THE DAY RUNS YOU.
>
> JIM ROHN

PRIORITISATION

Two words to consider are 'urgent' and 'important'. Urgent is how quickly something should be done, and important denotes the level of impact an item has upon your overall objectives. As a rule, it is the urgent tasks that are completed first and the more important tasks that are ignored (which, of course, eventually become important and urgent). Ever feel like all you are doing is fire fighting the everyday stuff and not getting to the high impact tasks? If so, then you probably need to review how you prioritise. A big lesson in this section is learning to say **'no'**, in the politest sense of course. In the busy world we live in as a leader, everyone wants a piece of you – your staff, your line manager, and other peers and colleagues. Do you let them prioritise your time?

Perhaps more importantly, **do you let others steal your time?** If you are not clear what your priorities are, in fact if you don't know what you hope to achieve today, tomorrow, or next week – then how do you know whether something new takes priority or not? Time to review both your commitments and those of your team, and placing them in order of priority is **paramount** if you want to build a fully effective team. The alternative is lots of headless chickens running around being very busy but not reaching their full potential.

Spend 10 minutes at the start of every day to think through what needs to be done, prioritise those needs, reallocate tasks, and schedule new ones – **this gives you a sense of control.** Then, when someone inevitably asks you to do something, you can make an informed decision based upon your understanding of time, need, control and priority. It really does work wonders – for you and your staff.

PRIME TIME

People have different body clocks, some are morning people and some work better in the afternoons. It doesn't matter when you work at your best; you just need to know when that is. This is what's called your **'prime time'.** When do you concentrate best? When are you more alert? When is your short term memory at its best? Generally, a large proportion of quality work is achieved in a relatively small amount of time. Therefore, you need to protect and insulate that time against intrusion. If you are a morning person, don't use those 2 hours of 'prime time' dealing with the tasks that are not important or don't take any thought, because in the afternoon, when you have that tough report to write, it will take you twice as long.

TIME BANDITS

Those things that steal your time without you knowing it such as emails, interruptions, and procrastination. Many of these regular things will steal much, much more of your time than you think. Overall, the aim is to understand how much of your day is actually tied up. There's no point in planning five hours of a seven hour day when four are already committed to things that are out of your hands! Knowing how much time (on average) is actually available to you each day allows you to plan effectively and not over-commit – which is where the activity log comes in!

It all comes down to **discipline.** Throughout the many workshops I deliver on precisely this subject, people all say “I’m a convert - I can make a difference with just a few small changes” – but it is so easy to slide back into bad habits – or even worse, fail to find the time to put the changes into practice!

What’s more, if you don’t put good time management principles into place, how can you expect your team to? Remember to **help your staff to manage their time more effectively.** Just think how much more productive, effective and efficient your team would be if you and every team member could each save 1 hour a day.

KEY WORDS
TO TIME MANAGEMENT

OBJECTIVES
PROCRASTINATION
PRIME TIME
DISCIPLINE
PLANNING
IMPORTANT
TIME BANDITS
URGENT
PRIORITISATION
PERSONAL
RESPONSIBILITY

TIME MANAGEMENT TIPS FOR THE BUS

- Set **clear** objectives (SMART) – be clear about your route and all other relevant information before leaving the depot
- Take 10 minutes to **plan** your day – even if deviations happen, you will quickly and easily know how to get back on the correct route
- Prioritise your work – what has to be done today, what you can delegate to others – how do you ensure that you get to the end of the journey on time with all stops visited? Remember, **'urgent'** & **'important'**
- Insulate your prime time – if you have a difficult route to negotiate, make certain you attempt it when you are at your best
- Don't let people steal your time – if you do, you will not meet the timetable

- Turn off the email flag - only check your emails when you are parked, which will allow you to check a number of them together - you certainly don't want to be stopping the bus every 2 minutes, imagine how your passengers would feel

- **Control** interruptions - wait until the bus is parked. The passengers can then ask you as many questions as they need to - surprisingly enough, they will become fewer as they lose patience in waiting and will go find the answers for themselves (empowerment, challenge & learning for the passengers)

- **Stop procrastinating** - if the bus has to be taken in for a repair, don't keep putting it off, make a plan to do it as soon as possible and stick to it. If not, it will certainly become much worse.

- Keep a clean, organised bus – rubbish, paper etc. is not only a health hazard, it makes it very difficult for passengers to move about, find things etc.
- **Discipline** for you and your passengers – adhere to the time management principles even when the going gets tough, don't try to cut corners that the bus might not make it round
- Set an example that your team can follow – hopefully, when you are not there, the bus will continue on its route as the team follows your examples

CHAPTER 8
DELEGATION

> "THE BEST EXECUTIVE IS THE ONE WHO HAS SENSE ENOUGH TO PICK GOOD MEN TO DO WHAT HE WANTS DONE, AND SELF-RESTRAINT ENOUGH TO KEEP FROM MEDDLING WITH THEM WHILE THEY DO IT."
>
> THEODORE ROOSEVELT

Delegation is one of the more difficult skills a new leader has to develop. We have to remember that most of the time individuals are promoted because they were excellent at the job they were doing. That almost certainly means they were effective, accurate, knowledgeable, technically brilliant, and probably better than anyone else in the department.

However, now that you are leading the team, your role is both to utilise and transfer those skills and knowledge to bring members of your team up to that same standard. The concept is perfect, so why do many managers find it so difficult? Here are some regularly cited reasons:

- They simply haven't got the time
- It is quicker to do it themselves
- They are the only one that knows how
- If you want a good job doing - do it yourself
- They don't trust the staff
- They think the staff members/team don't possess the skills
- They are reluctant to share their knowledge
- Status/Ego

Yes, I used many of those reasons too! But what we have to remember is that **effective** delegation helps you to get work done through other people – the **main** task for any leader. This is vital if we are to maintain the flexibility needed to adapt to the ever changing world in which we live.

So let's look at why delegation is a good idea. First of all, there's the benefit to the people to whom we delegate. Delegation allows your team to develop new skills and competencies at a higher level as well as increase their knowledge through access to new sources of information. This shows trust, recognition, and value; it empowers them, provides experience and, most importantly, opportunities to shine. Delegation is also **hugely motivational.** Added responsibility will tend to increase commitment to the leader, the task and ultimately the team.

This is leadership at its best, and a key role in your job.

> "SURROUND YOURSELF WITH THE BEST PEOPLE YOU CAN FIND, DELEGATE AUTHORITY, AND DON'T INTERFERE."
>
> RONALD REAGAN

Staff who are competent, involved, committed, and well informed are much more likely to perform well. This ensures that they add real value to the organisation and, incidentally, makes them easier and less time-consuming to manage! Good delegation also helps the leader take a step back, look at the bigger picture and, therefore, make better decisions.

In teams where delegation is effective, there is a better flow of information up and down – leading to better planning, organisation and control. It helps us to make the most of our time. Even if we just delegate the low and medium priority tasks, we will have more time for the work that **really** impacts and influences the wider outcomes of the team.

Proper delegation also increases the span of control, helping us to lead bigger teams, which is an important factor in today's flatter organisations. Finally, it can improve overall team performance, building on individual strengths and commitment, and increases confidence, which in turn develops their weaker areas. This again demonstrates confidence in your team and increases the pool of skills available to you in the long term.

And, yes, in the short term it will take more time than if you did it yourself - time spent training, coaching and supporting – but they will get quicker! Remember when you learnt the task, you took longer too.

As an example, take a task that needs to be carried out weekly for an hour, 52 weeks of the year. It may take you four times longer to train someone else once rather than do it yourself. However, that short term loss only amounts to 3 hours, which means over the course of the year you've gained 48 hours!

> **Think of it as an investment: in the long term, it really isn't quicker to do it yourself.**

Clearly, however, there are some things we just shouldn't delegate – personal matters for a start. Any leader has to maintain a level of control that matches your preferred approach to management, the skills, experience and, of course, the attitude of your staff. Then there are the constraints of the job to be considered. If the work is highly risky in some way, or there are clear rules forbidding it, obviously you can't delegate. At the end of the day it's a balance, and this balance relates to the level of **control** required, and the level of **trust** you have in the likelihood that a good job will be done. Seek to push control and decision-making as far down as possible, wherever possible. That way we gain the advantage.

> NEVER TELL PEOPLE HOW TO DO THINGS. TELL THEM WHAT TO DO AND THEY WILL SURPRISE YOU WITH THEIR INGENUITY.
>
> GEORGE S. PATTON

If you think you are already a good delegator, apply this test: when you come back from holiday, do you have loads of work and unresolved issues to deal with? If so, there's a pretty good chance that you're not delegating as effectively as you could be.

Really, there are six key steps to effective delegation:

DECIDE WHAT NEEDS TO BE DONE

Exactly what is it that you're delegating? Have you ensured the clarity and measurability of your objective? Who are you going to delegate to? Why this person? What is the benefit to you and them? Must you always delegate to the same person or the person who possesses the most knowledge? Are there other advantages to delegating to someone else **(advancement, motivation, opportunity to praise, making someone feel valued, inclusion etc.)**? Do they need training? Will you train them? Can someone else (advancement for another team member possibly)? Do you or they require examples, extra resources, extra time and so on?

In simple terms, **do not shoot from the hip:** plan what, why, how, when, where and to whom before you move onto the next step.

COMMUNICATE CLEARLY

Consider the lesson from Chapter 2 – two way communication. Ensure the individual fully understands the objective. Break into bite-sized chunks and ask them questions to encourage initiative, rather than simply telling them what you want them to do. One of the main reasons delegation fails so often is that the leader has not explained themselves clearly. If you have completed step one effectively, step two should be much easier to achieve.

SUMMARISE

Before you let the individual go, ensure they have clearly summarised what **you expect of them and what they can expect from you.** Don't ask "do you understand" and take "yes" as the answer. Ask questions such as "what is your first step?", "what happens next?", "who will you seek help from?" etc. until you're confident that they really do understand what it is that they need to achieve and how. A step that is regularly missed if the individual has not fully understood it will cost you time, either in returning to the task or in revisiting a dissatisfied client.

AGREE UPON A TIMEFRAME

Not just for completion of the task but for how often you are going to meet to support, help and encourage the individual as well as personally monitor that the task is on track. Of course, **this will differ with every team member;** some learn quicker than others, some have more or less confidence, and some just need different levels of support. This must be agreed upon **before** you both move onto the next step. However, though you may need a degree of comfort, remember that this is more about the individual than it is about you. It may be more than you are used to giving, but decide how much space the individual needs in order to flourish with confidence. This is the balance of **control** and trust – a very difficult skill to master when first playing the role of the delegator.

LET GO AND TRUST

If the previous four steps have been completed successfully, both parties should be confident to move forward and achieve what has been agreed. **Do not break the agreed timetable** (or watch over their shoulder and micromanage). You risk knocking their confidence, they won't feel trusted and may lose their motivation - all the things you were hoping to achieve by delegating to this person in the first place.

REWARD SUCCESSFUL COMPLETION

This is always easy if the task has been completed successfully, but please don't forget or be too busy to do it. **Delegation is the most motivational tool in the leader's toolbox.** It gives you the opportunity to make people feel valued, enthused, included, and it makes people grow in confidence. Even if the task is not fully completed, there is **always** room for praise, however small. Remember, when you learnt the task however many years ago you probably didn't get it right first time either.

So in a nutshell, delegation, if done correctly, is a very powerful tool and the more effective you are at delegating the more effective and successful your team will be. Do it ineffectively and it can be a very dangerous undertaking. So I implore you to take the time, plan, execute and do it for the right reasons – the benefit of the individual, the team, the organisation and you.

KEY WORDS IN DELEGATION

DEVELOPMENT
TWO-WAY COMMUNICATION
VALUED
MOTIVATION
TRUSTED
CLARITY
EXPECTATION
PRAISE
EMPOWERED
TIME FRAME
ACHIEVEMENT
STRETCH

DELEGATION TIPS FOR THE BUS

Before, during and after
the bus journey:

- Never delegate tasks without planning (it doesn't always need to take a long time)
- Think why you are delegating to someone – what are the benefits to the individual, you, the team & the organisation?
- Can another team member provide support? Does it always have to be you? (great development for other passengers)
- Break every instruction into bite-sized chunks (see Chapter 10)
- Don't ever just dump jobs
- Try and delegate advancement tasks as well as offloading everyday menial work

- If you ever think you don't have time – calculate how much time you spend doing that task over a year – then work out how long it would take you (or someone else) to train another
- Follow the six stage process
- Delegate and have motivated, empowered, challenged and inspired passengers on your bus

CHAPTER 9
PERFORMANCE MANAGEMENT

> "Goals are the fuel in the furnace of achievement."
>
> Brian Tracy

I absolutely believe that performance management is an important activity for a leader, and that it is key to getting the best out of our people. If we accept that our role as a leader is to support, develop, empower and challenge our staff, then we accept that performance management (done properly) is the tool for making it happen.

But if you want it to work, **both parties must want to take an active part** and follow some key principles. This chapter explores those key principles and examines just how to put them into action.

Before we begin, we must note that performance management has to start with the alignment of your corporate strategy and business plan. Once the overall goals of the company are agreed it is then paramount that all staff:

- Know what is expected of them during the year
- Have clear and **agreed** standards to measure how well they've done
- Know what support will be available to help them achieve
- Know how the achievement of their objectives will contribute to the team, the department and the company

The first key principle is that performance management is not about the paperwork, ticking boxes on forms or keeping HR happy! It's about helping leaders and their staff to understand and agree exactly what each individual is going to contribute to fulfilling the company's goals.

Done well, performance management helps to clarify individual goals, motivate people through challenging objectives, and have effective development plans in place to support those objectives.

> **It clearly shows what success will look like, confirms individual (and team) training needs, feeds into succession planning, and allows consistency across teams and departments.**

At the very least, performance management offers an opportunity to praise and/or pull up, and ensures the best use of development resources.

Just ask yourself: wouldn't you prefer to know exactly what is expected of you (clear objectives), what success looks like (exactly the criteria you will be measured on), and what support you will be given to meet what should be stretching objectives? Wouldn't you like to have a plan for your future career development? If the answer is yes to all the above, then performance management is the way to go – for you and for your team.

Unfortunately, what passes for performance management for many people has been a negative experience. For line managers it can be a bureaucratic chore that takes up a lot of time for little return on the investment. For staff it can feel like criticism, an opportunity to highlight the negative. But it really shouldn't be that way.

> "IF YOU DON'T KNOW WHERE YOU ARE GOING, YOU'LL END UP SOMEPLACE ELSE."
>
> YOGI BERRA

Firstly, let's look at who should own the responsibility. Who is it about, and whose job and career development is it? Who is measured against the objectives? Very clearly, the answer is the individual.

> **The individual should own, and the line manager should support.**

So how should it work? It's really very simple:

- **Plan and define the priorities and standards of performance**
- **Plan the support needed to achieve delivery**
- **Review performance against the agreed measures**

The second key principle is that this is a two-way process, which means communication is the foundation of performance management. Both the line manager and the individual need to be able to have open, honest and frank conversations about expectations, support, and so forth. This is not about the line manager imposing their will on the staff member (this is very poor performance management), it's about negotiation and discussion to achieve:

- Mutually agreed and understood expectations about future performance
- An accepted and balanced review of current performance
- A clear plan to meet development needs

Another key principle is that good performance management is a 24/7 concern. It is not just the formal process of periodic official meetings to set objectives, fill out forms, review performance, evaluate training, etc. (however vital those parts might be). Equally as important is the 'business as usual' aspect - what happens on a daily basis such as coaching, delegation, feedback, and all the other things that good leaders do to support, motivate and train their people. This is the key component that makes performance management successful. See the diagram below.

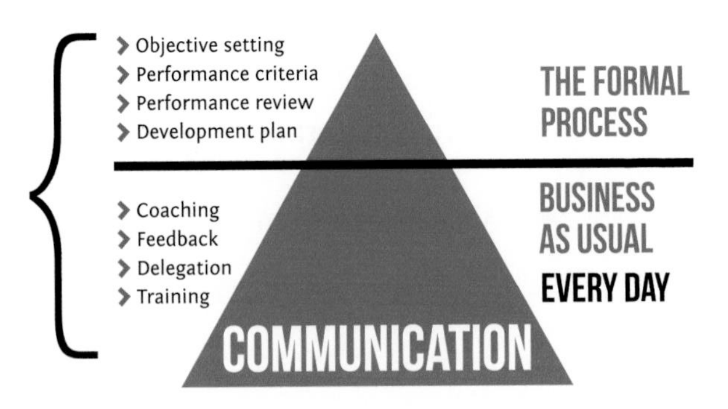

Let's look at it another way: if you have some issues, need support, or simply need to check how well you're doing, you don't want to wait 6 months to find out whether or not you've been successful. In 6 months' time, it will be too late! Surely discussing these things as and when they arise will offer an opportunity for both parties to put them right and get the support needed to make the agreed changes. That way leads to success and ultimate achievement at the formal review, with no surprises for anyone. As your line manager I would certainly want you to be talking to me, so that I can help and support you to achieve - **because if you fail, I fail.**

The most effective organisations take their strategy and build corporate objectives to deliver it. That done, they then feed them down through division, department, section and into individual objectives – each one fitting like the pieces of a jigsaw to complete the bigger picture. This way, every single person's objectives are contributing in some direct way to the achievement of the overall strategy. Very useful, obviously, and not difficult to do when the focus for your performance management process is improvement for the future, rather than a post-mortem of the past - **effective performance management only uses the past to inform the future.**

> "GOALS IN WRITING ARE DREAMS WITH DEADLINES."
>
> BRIAN TRACY

So let's talk about setting objectives. The first rule (in my opinion) is that no-one should have more than 4, maybe 5 objectives. To narrow them down, focus on things that are absolutely critical to the job, or where improvement is required (and possible), all the while making sure that they are within the power of the individual to achieve – albeit with a little help. Job descriptions are often a good place to start, as they usually say what a person is supposed to be doing. Try to group things together and use common tasks as measures of success for those broader objectives. Overleaf is an example, should the delivery of customer service be a core part of the job role.

Objective: To deliver an excellent level of customer service.

On its own, this objective is not specific enough, and would be impossible to measure. So we must have a range of measures to clarify this objective, for example:

- All correspondence sent to the client must be 100% accurate
- No more than 1 official complaint in 6 months
- Seek formal feedback from 2 clients per month
- All clients must have received a return contact within 24 hours
- Adhere to the formal department standards set

Now we can see that the objective and its underlying measures **together** create a relevant and measurable goal. You don't need to reinvent the wheel if standards are already set, as long as they are clear and well understood - just refer to them. There are 2 types of measures:

- **QUANTITATIVE** measures, which are mostly about what you do - how many, how long, how much. These are the simplest and most used measures.
- **QUALITATIVE** measures, which tend to be about how you do things. Often based on behaviour, these are more difficult so people unfortunately tend to avoid them.

To provide a working example: suppose you have a very technically competent team member who can answer all client queries, hits all deadlines, and never misses a day's work. However, whenever he speaks to clients, he comes across as abrupt, uninterested and off-hand. Without qualitative measures, you would be unable to pick up these behavioural issues which will certainly be costing you clients. You may also be storing up bigger problems should you choose to promote that individual as a result of their high technical performance.

Objectives should also be **stretching.** Let's say that an individual easily achieved a target last year of 20 widgets an hour - you may want to increase this year's measure to 23, 24, or 25. Of course, you must make objectives achievable or people won't bother trying, but if they're too easy then people become bored and complacent. And don't forget: **discuss and negotiate - this is a two-way communication process.**

The overriding point is that we are unlikely to achieve objectives if we haven't got any. Every business has high level objectives, so the question has to be how well those objectives are shared with the people who have to deliver them. As a line manager, you have to be absolutely clear about what your boss expects from you, because if you aren't, how can you set clear expectations for your staff?

With clear objectives and measures set, deciding upon training needs and priorities becomes an easy exercise. Simply consider the knowledge, experience, behaviour and skills needed to achieve the objectives, and identify any shortfalls - **a straightforward case of deduction.** However, we also need to look further ahead than just this year's objectives, and consider longer term career planning over, say, the next 5 years. This will help you with your succession planning and may also help you to understand the individual's longer term aims and objectives. Support those and you build **commitment** and **motivation.**

Most importantly, talk to your people regularly and give them feedback all the time - there should never be any surprises for either party at formal review meetings. If you do the 'business as usual' as part of the job, then the formal meetings become just an official opportunity to clarify points, confirm outcomes and document future steps. For the line manager, it's all about praising achievement, recognising growth, and resolving issues through whatever support may be required.

So who should do most of the talking at your meetings? Without a doubt, it should be the individual. It is they who should have a clear idea (and evidence!) of what they have done well and not so well. If anyone comes out of a formal review meeting surprised or shocked at the outcome, then performance management is not being carried out effectively.

All leaders need to motivate and inspire their staff to **want** to be part of this process. If they don't feel that way yet, then we need to find out why and actively sell the benefits.

> **Performance management works best when individuals take personal responsibility for continuously improving their own performance.**

That's it – performance management made simple. If you're not doing it, how do you know whether you're doing the right things to achieve your aims? And how will you know what to fix if you're not?

KEY WORDS IN PERFORMANCE MANAGEMENT

PERSONAL RESPONSIBILITY

OWNERSHIP

OBJECTIVES

TWO-WAY COMMUNICATION

DEVELOPMENT

MOTIVATION

24/7

CONSISTENCY

MEASUREMENT

STRETCH

FEEDBACK

PRAISE/PULL-UP

PERFORMANCE MANAGEMENT TIPS FOR THE BUS

- Set clear objectives – do you know where the bus is going?
- Are the objectives measurable? If not, they are not objectives
- Agree the objectives with the passengers – get their input
- Are they written down? If not, they should be
- Do the objectives reflect the individual, team and organisation's needs? You shouldn't be leaving the bus station until they do

- Include a plan for any support, training, etc. that might be needed – allow time for the passengers to get off the bus and participate in what has been agreed
- Regularly check to see how the passengers are doing against the objectives so that you can change course if required
- **Don't be too busy driving the bus** to remember coaching and mentoring – the day-to-day support required to make performance management a success

CHAPTER 10
DEVELOPING OTHERS

> "LEADERSHIP AND LEARNING ARE INDISPENSABLE TO EACH OTHER."
>
> JOHN F. KENNEDY

As we discussed in Chapter 1, leaders need to challenge, stretch, inspire and motivate their staff, as well as offer praise, give feedback, and make them feel valued. All of these are important ways to enable people to work collectively and individually to achieve their own objectives and those of the team.

But we also need to ensure that people are sufficiently skilled and competent enough to carry out their role. Leaders, therefore, need to develop their team.

Before we have a look at ways to develop our staff efficiently and effectively, let's have a look at some reasons leaders don't always achieve success in this key area.

Lack of time

Lack of resource

Lack of knowledge

Don't know where to get help and advice themselves

Sometimes just a lack of understanding that part of a leader's role is to develop those that work for them.

If any of these sound familiar then the first step as a leader is to address these issues before we move on to those of your team. Leaders must always look at the bigger picture. To develop our staff does indeed take time, money and often scarce resources, but ultimately this is a **long term investment.** Lack of investment may result in your team becoming (or staying) de-motivated, bored, uncooperative and complacent, never more competent or efficient than they are today. All of this impacts your ability to deliver for the organisation and the customer. Even if you have a highly successful team at present, without further investment you will find it very difficult to maintain that level of success.

Let's look at a couple of simple examples:

John has been on paternity leave for one year and has returned to work in his old role. Of course he needs an update on a few changes that have happened in his absence and a briefing on any new products. You planned to spend a few hours with him to explain. Through the usual pressure of work, that didn't happen on his return and two weeks later a very important client called with a highly technical question about one of the new products. You were out of the office and John couldn't answer any of the client's questions. I wonder how much that cost compared to the time you might have spent with John?

Let's try another. For the past year you intended to teach Kay how to complete the monthly report that collates all team salaries and overtime payments. For one good reason or another, you hadn't quite gotten round to it and you are now off sick for at least 3 months. As Kay does not know how to complete the task, all 20 staff will receive a basic salary, which will have a significant effect on their motivation and goodwill. Without the investment of time in Kay (it would have taken you 3 hours in total to have trained her), neither she nor anyone else can help.

To be honest, both of these are examples of **poor management,** particularly of poor time management, but they also show how often the task of developing others is assigned as a low priority. Both cases demonstrate very bad judgement on behalf of the leader, with consequences that could have been avoided with the proper development of others. What's more, organisations that develop their people tend to save money on recruitment by having better rates of retention – especially when it comes to those who can choose where they work (usually the best people).

Apart from improving skills and knowledge, **your capacity to help others develop is also one of the key motivational tools that you have in your armoury,** and should not be dismissed. Assuming you now accept that to be true, let's have a look at ways to make development easier, more efficient, and successful.

When we talk about developing staff we are not just talking about training courses. Courses may be one answer, but there are lots of other ways to expand a person's horizons. **Coaching, shadowing, secondment, projects, guided self-learning and, don't forget, delegation** are often much better options when you need to develop specific company skills, or enhance their understanding of the role, processes, or products. Even if direct training is the answer, these things will often need to be taught on the job, at their desk and on a 1-2-1 basis. For many, particularly new team leaders, you were probably promoted initially because you were technically fantastic, even superb, at precisely the things that you now want others to do for you. That makes you the best person to teach others, to pass over all that knowledge and experience so your staff can develop. As importantly, these two go hand in hand, so as your staff develop, so can you (see Chapter 8).

> “IF YOUR ACTIONS INSPIRE OTHERS TO DREAM MORE, LEARN MORE, DO MORE AND BECOME MORE, YOU ARE A LEADER.”
>
> JOHN QUINCY ADAMS

I must have seen what I call ‘the sit by Nelly technique’ – you sit, I show, I leave, you do - hundreds of times and not once have I seen it be wholly successful.

The Nelly technique fails for many reasons:

> **it provides little or no thought to the learner, no planning and preparation, no logical progression, too much information in one sitting, becomes too rushed, is littered with interruptions, invites a lack of focus, provides no foundation for understanding and passes over bad habits, to name but a few.**

I could go on, but the basic problem is that 'Nelly', expert though she is, either does not know, or chooses not to adhere to, the following key principles.

Before we begin, remember that, as with anything important and time consuming, you only want to do it once. That means doing it properly, that means planning and preparation, and that means thinking it through. There are four key areas that you need to take into account:

PLANNING

Be clear and specific about what you are teaching

Set an objective – what, how much, by when? – be realistic

Make the objective measurable – how else will you evaluate success?

Write it down

THE STRUCTURE

Decide the main headings, and what to cover under each heading

Prepare some notes – the more expert you are, the more you need notes to ensure that you leave nothing out

What methods and aids will you use? Case studies? Examples? Reference material?

Build in checks

What follow-up will you put in place to check success once the training has been delivered?

LEARNER

What knowledge and experience do they already have? Don't assume - check

What is their preferred learning style? Ask them - it may be different to yours – then change your approach accordingly

PREPARATION

Yourself - book the time out of your diary

Environment – distractions, phones, interruptions, etc. – seek support from others

Materials – paperwork, systems, visual aids, etc.

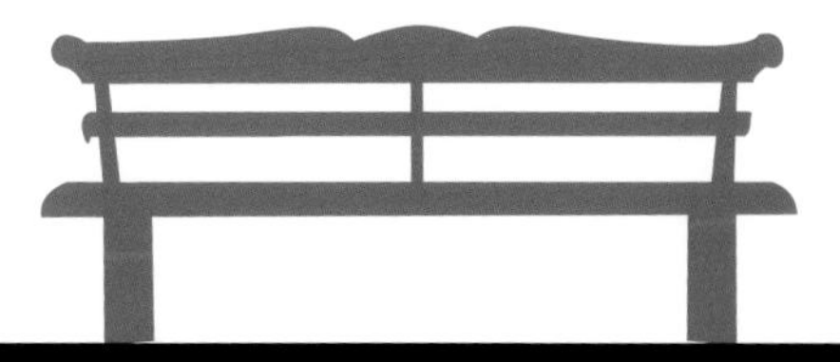

These guidelines are fairly comprehensive in their approach, however there are a couple of other things that you need to think about.

For a start, you need to ensure that the training progresses logically for the learner. It may be that the order in which you have to complete a task is not the easiest way to learn it, so it really pays to give some thought to the order in which you need to deliver the information. This is what we call the A-Z of learning. This is to ensure that it makes sense to the learner and that they can learn in the most effective and efficient way for them, not you.

Think also about how much information a learner can absorb in one go. Make sure that you don't overload them with too much and, wherever possible, work in **bite-sized chunks** – it's simply more digestible. It also helps if you give the student time to think things over. Try delivering a small chunk of information, check their understanding, then let them have a go and be successful before you move on to the next chunk. This technique meets two requirements: evaluation of learning (which means you only teach them once) and regular breaks to maintain focus (we only have about 20-30 minutes of serious focus time).

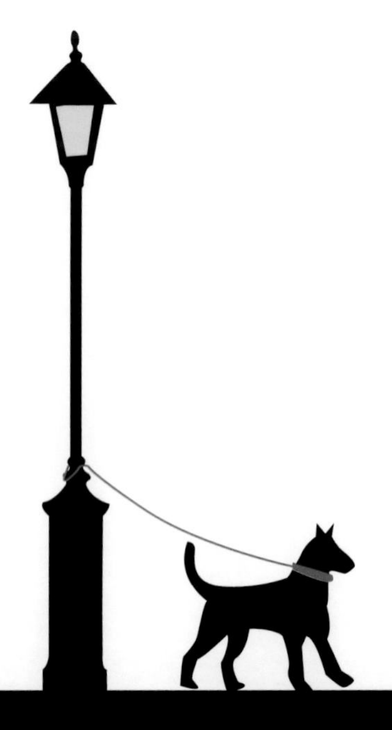

Finally, try to **maintain their interest with a variety of learning methods.** We learn much more quickly if we are interested, motivated, allowed to participate (don't talk at them) and, if possible, allowed to **have fun.** Difficult as that may be, when you are teaching someone a new administration process while under time pressure, the more you follow these suggestions the easier it will be.

Please don't think it's all over once you've finished the preliminary training! Follow up with the learner to make sure that they have retained and can use what they have learned. Coach to further develop their new skills and offer continued support in case of difficulty or uncertainty. These considerations really come into their own only after the training itself has been completed.

Above all, be patient and **allow learners to make mistakes** (people learn a lot by doing something wrong). I'm sure your own mistakes have helped you to learn along the way. Have a little empathy and remember that what you are good at today was not always so easy. Something that has helped me in the past is to remember when someone took the time to teach me something that I excel at today. It always makes me want to give someone else the same opportunity.

Development is a key motivational tool for leaders, so remember praise and feedback.

> **This is the ideal opportunity to praise your staff, to empower them to try new things, to give them appropriate autonomy, and to lead them to the top of that motivational curve (Chapter 4).**

If you as a leader can find time to develop your staff then they grow, you grow, and the whole team becomes even more successful. The next step is for the team members themselves to follow your example and help to train and develop each other by passing over their knowledge and experience (in the same correct manner, of course). With that in place, just imagine the type of open, honest, positive, motivated culture that all team members will enjoy on the bus.

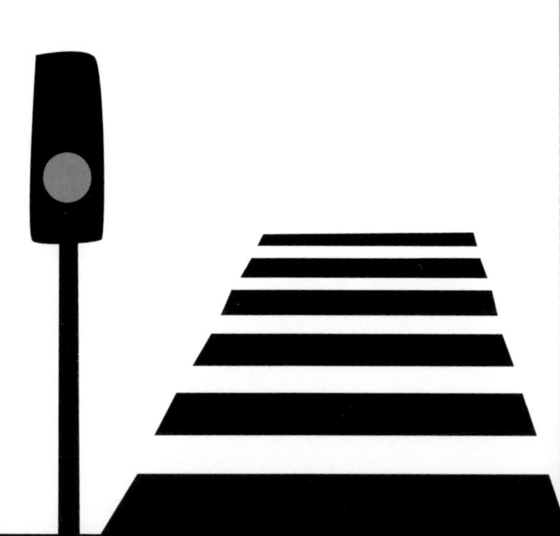

KEY WORDS IN DEVELOPING OTHERS

FUN
PREPARATION
FEEDBACK
LOGICAL PROGRESSION
EVALUATION
PRAISE
MOTIVATION
FOLLOW UP
VARIETY
PLANNING
BITE-SIZED CHUNKS

DEVELOPING OTHERS TIPS FOR THE BUS

- Planning & Preparation – let others on the bus know what you are doing - in fact, seek their assistance if you can
- As a key motivational tool, try to find learning and development opportunities for all the passengers
- Small, bite-sized chunks – evaluate before moving on
- Make the learning interesting and **fun** – use a variety of methods
- Find reasons to develop your staff - not excuses for why you can't
- Don't just have them 'sit by Nelly' – give the learner the opportunity to learn properly the first time round
- If you want a highly successful bus journey, make certain you have **skilled, competent and motivated passengers onboard**

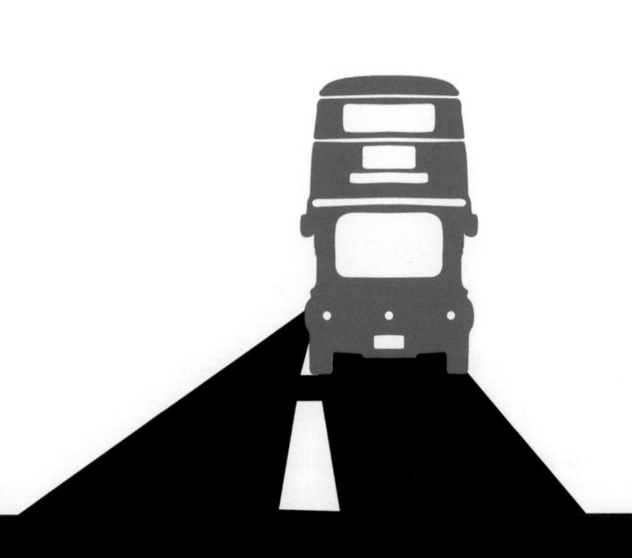

CHAPTER 11
PERSONAL RESPONSIBILITY

> "HAPPINESS IS NOT BY CHANCE, BUT BY CHOICE."
>
> JIM ROHN

Personal responsibility is all about an individual's willingness to take ownership and responsibility for their actions, behaviours and, importantly, their choices. This sounds so obvious that we shouldn't even need to discuss it – doesn't everyone take responsibility for what they do? Well, no. In the real world that is unfortunately not always the case, so let's have a look at why that might be.

The first question we should ask is "what **must** we do?" Apart from breathing, what do we absolutely have to do? Choice is at the heart of personal responsibility: you make a choice and you are responsible for it - which all sounds very simple! Unfortunately, it is what happens after someone has made a choice that counts, in terms of how much responsibility they are prepared to own.

The problem is that all choices have consequences, and people often make choices based on our emotional needs (fear of the consequences, for example), rather than on what they would actually prefer to do or what they think is right. We can't always choose the situation in which we find ourselves, but we can **always** choose how we respond to it. It is about taking responsibility for the choice that we make (whatever the reasons for that choice are), taking ownership of it, and accepting the consequences of our decision.

> “ THIS IS YOUR LIFE. YOU ARE RESPONSIBLE FOR IT. YOU WILL NOT LIVE FOREVER. DON'T WAIT. ”
>
> NATALIE GOLDBERG

This really happened: I was listening to someone as they complained to me about their job. They hated it, loathed getting up to go to work, and generally felt that they were wasting their life. At work, I had heard they were miserable, argumentative and unhelpful to their colleagues who, unsurprisingly, reacted badly to that behaviour. Overall then, life was awful, work was awful, life was completely unfair, but what could they do? Nothing at all, in their view. My reaction to this tale of woe was that they needed to take personal responsibility for their choices. They **chose** (for whatever reason) to keep going to this particular job, so they should either quit and accept the consequences, or stop blaming others and make the best of what they've got.

Neither option is ideal (as is often the case), but what matters is to recognise that it was our choice, to be okay with that, and to make the best of the result. Blaming the world for your choices just makes you unhappy because you feel powerless - and unhappy people tend to make others unhappy. If the individual **accepted ownership** then hopefully they could look at the positives, find some motivation and decide that it was up to them to take the lead rather than blaming everyone else for where they were.

So what do I mean by 'blame'? When somebody won't take responsibility, as far as they're concerned the consequences of their choices are anybody's fault but their own. They tend to see themselves as one of life's victims, and so they make some of the excuses below (I'm sure you've never used any of these):

- "I've got to..."
- "I had no choice..."
- "I didn't have the time..."
- "I've been forced to..."
- "I'm doing this for you..."

- "I can't turn up..."
- "I must do this..."
- "I have to do that..."
- "See what you made me do..."
- "He kept me talking..."
- "I'd rather be somewhere else..."
- "I accepted against my will..."

All of the above are about making excuses for choices someone doesn't want to own – which is easier if you can blame someone else. Can you imagine being part of a team of people that use this kind of language all the time? Is that the sort of bus that you would want to be on? The culture would be one of blame, negativity, lack of motivation, all with no support, and I would want no part of it.

When we link personal responsibility to the line manager, we must think about the choices that we offer our team members. Leaders should never try to manipulate, use guilt, or force people into choices. Your team may do what you ask but they will not feel responsible for the task at hand. When it all goes wrong they will certainly not be telling you about it, much less putting up their hands to say it was their fault. As a result, not only will you have cultivated a blame culture but you will also have lost all openness, honesty and trust.

> **Far better to have people do things out of principled choice.**

> "THIS I CHOOSE TO DO. IF THERE IS A PRICE, THIS I CHOOSE TO PAY."
>
> TERRY PRATCHETT

So how do we develop a **culture** of personal responsibility?

Firstly, we have to lead by example. As line managers we all need to make choices that we would prefer not to make, from a range of options for which we don't care. For example, the powers-that-be may make decisions with which we don't agree. So what're your options? Having made your case, you can either refuse (which might cost you your job) or you can do. The point is, if you don't feel strongly enough to quit over something, then you have **chosen** to do it, and that choice means that you should take it onboard positively, taking your people with you. If you don't, then your team is not going to buy in to the task, and that is a clear route to failure which will be down to you.

> BE MISERABLE. OR MOTIVATE YOURSELF. WHATEVER HAS TO BE DONE, IT'S ALWAYS YOUR CHOICE.
>
> WAYNE DYER

I have two sayings that I think put personal responsibility into real context:

> **"I accept without complaint full personal responsibility for the choices I make in life."**

> **"I am where I am because of the choices I have made."**

If all of us were to accept the truth of these statements, and act accordingly by taking ownership of our actions and behaviours, imagine what type of culture you would have on your bus.

But how do you help yourself and your team take personal responsibility? It's simple, by our actions and through a set of key principles:

Honesty, Integrity, Justice, Consideration, Loyalty Sincerity, Courage

When the going gets tough and you have to make difficult choices from bad options, then making the choice based on those principles will help. To base decisions on principle rather than fear of the consequences, however, takes real courage; the courage to stand your ground, to be honest, to make the tough choice even if it makes people unhappy. If you can find the courage, then the results will always be better – and you'll know you did the right thing.

There's no need for excuses and other victim language when we take responsibility!

Nobody ever said that taking personal responsibility was easy, but if you can develop and encourage your team to do just that then, without a doubt, your bus will become more efficient, more successful and create an environment that others will want to be part of.

So what do **you** need to do? Firstly, have a general chat with your team - talk about what personal responsibility really is, or even give them this chapter to read. Then promote confidence and belief, adopt a positive mindset, be enthused and have a 'go for it' attitude. **Lead by example:** live by your principles and, however hard the consequences of a choice may be, face them with a smile on your face. Take out the negativity and stop the 'I had no choice' culture. Have the moral courage to make the tough decisions and to stand by them. Think about the impact your behaviour and mindset has on the members of your team. In simple terms, take personal responsibility for everything you do and promote the same in others.

Finally, after reading Chapter 12 on positive mindset, I hope you will see that these two chapters go hand in hand. When you are trying to take responsibility for your choices in difficult circumstances, your mindset makes all the difference.

KEY WORDS IN PERSONAL RESPONSIBILITY

CHOICE

NO BLAME

ENTHUSIASM

LOYALTY

CONSIDERATION

SINCERITY

POSITIVE

OWNERSHIP

HONESTY

INTEGRITY

COURAGE

SELF-CONFIDENCE

PERSONAL RESPONSIBILITY TIPS FOR THE BUS

- Lead by example - live by the principles of personal responsibility
- Foster a 'no blame' culture on your bus
- Encourage and support your team to take personal responsibility
- Don't put your staff in a position where guilt makes them unable to take personal responsibility
- Have the **moral courage** to make the tough choices and then follow them positively - encourage others to do the same
- Adopt a **positive mindset** for all choices that you make
- Recognise 'victim language' for what it is and don't allow it on the bus

CHAPTER 12
POSITIVE THINKING

> "MINDS ARE LIKE PARACHUTES - THEY ONLY FUNCTION WHEN OPEN."
>
> THOMAS DEWAR

A positive mindset affects how we feel, how we behave, and especially how we work. Thinking positively is absolutely the key driver of our attitude, motivation (Chapter 4), and achievement. So let's have a look at it generally, and first consider a simple question. How do you answer when someone asks:

> **"do you think this is possible?"**

Whatever 'this' is, how you react to such questions is important (especially for a leader). A positive answer says "go ahead" and encourages effort to achieve. A negative one says "don't even try, it'll be a waste of effort". Now don't get me wrong, a really poor idea needs to be closed down, but this needs to be achieved in a positive way, one that doesn't encourage negativity. Ultimately, the key point has to be whether or not your answer is based on a realistic assessment of the possibilities, or on fear - fear of failure, fear of the unknown, or any one of the many other things that provoke us to react negatively.

One way or another, the rational decision based upon sound judgement is positive. The negative decision, however, is defensive, rigid, and based on knee-jerk instinct. What we have to remember is that to make something happen – especially something new, difficult, or risky - you have to be positive and believe it can be done.

> **If you believe you will fail, then you probably will.**

Let's look at a simple example. You wake up in the morning 10 or 20 minutes late (if it's 2 hours late this analogy won't work for you, you're stuffed!). You think: "Oh no, I'm going to be late, by the time I've done everything I'll have missed the train..." and your mindset changes. You convince yourself that nothing can be done, that the day is going to be a disaster, and that every decision you take will be coloured by that negativity – all based on something that hasn't happened yet!

Alternatively, you could say to yourself: "right, what do I need to do to make that train?" In that state of mind you will make a plan to achieve that goal. Change your morning routine (forget the caffeine fix - you can have it later), do your make-up on the train, whatever, and you will unconsciously speed up. Now if you make the train, great; you got there and everything's golden. But even if you don't, the positive mindset makes it much less of a downer and you move on to Plan B. By the way, if you **are** two hours late, you can either feel bad about it or choose to make the best of a bad job. Positive thinking again.

Here's another example. I work with individuals at all levels who are unemployed and don't want to be. Before they go for an interview, my first question is always: "do you believe you have a chance of being offered the role?". When someone says 'no', I tell them not to bother going. Why? Because if they believe there is no chance of success, it will show. A negative mindset leads to low confidence and a lack of self-belief, and that will manifest itself in their body language, in the way they present themselves, and in the way they communicate.

> **If you believe that you don't deserve anything, that you are not good enough, and that nothing good can happen to you, other people are very likely to believe it too.**

Believing you have a chance has a subtle but important effect on your behaviour: you may plan more, do some research, walk a bit taller, look and act more confident, ask good questions, sell your strengths, and ultimately send a strong signal that you are motivated and want the role on offer. Of course, these things don't guarantee success, but they do massively increase your chances.

> **People are more likely to believe in someone who obviously believes in themselves.**

> I DO NOT BELIEVE IN TAKING THE RIGHT DECISION, I TAKE A DECISION AND MAKE IT RIGHT.
>
> MUHAMMAD ALI JINNAH

Following on from Chapter 11, Personal Responsibility, remember that only you control how you think and feel. I know that sometimes it can seem like others are influencing you, but at the end of the day they can only do so if you let them. Now, I don't promise success and I'm not much of a theorist, but for me it's just a question of logic: if you believe something can happen, then you can influence the outcome. The real question is whether you are influencing the outcome **positively or negatively.** Let's have a look at the differences between a positive and negative mindset.

The key driver of a negative mindset is fear. Fear affects our attitude to risk and, therefore, our willingness to try anything new. If we are driven by that fear then it affects our confidence and self-belief, which in turn affects how we behave.

On the other hand, a positive mindset gives us a 'go for it' attitude to uncertainty, which allows us to try new things and, whether through success or failure, to grow in confidence and learn.

So how can we impact and influence our own mindset? Firstly, we must acknowledge that there are two key aspects to being positive:

1. **You have to want to be**
2. **You have to be self-aware**

The more we understand ourselves and how we react to things, the more we can influence our own mindset. Of course, what happens around us has an effect on how we feel, and we often have no control over the circumstances in which we find ourselves. But if we can look at them rationally (and not allow ourselves to be driven by fear) then we can better choose the way in which we deal with the situation and take positive steps towards a better outcome.

As I said earlier, we might not always get the outcome we wanted.

> **However, if we don't believe there is any chance of success then we will never try, and if we don't try then we can never succeed.**

Instead, we end up in a vicious cycle of negativity and the longer we stay within that negative cycle, the harder it is to break out of it.

The next time you convince yourself that you're going to fail, think about the impact of that negative mindset:

- You won't try to find a solution – because you know you're going to fail
- You won't bother to try – what's the point if you're going to fail anyway?
- Why do anything new when you've failed before?
- You get very grumpy and aggressive (or quiet and withdrawn) when people tell you it's possible – because you know it isn't

- We can always find an excuse, or blame something else (Chapter 11)
- Finally, we accept failure without even trying
- You are now part of the negative mindset cycle

So how do you **break the cycle?** I recommend a good stiff word with yourself. Let's try it:

- You are going to succeed – because you believe it is possible and you want to
- You will look for alternative solutions – break the habit
- Try a little bit harder – sometimes that's all it takes
- You've succeeded before – so you can again

- Failure is not failure – it's a way of learning how not to do something
- You are now more willing to seek help or advice – you're open to new approaches and ideas
- You want to feel good about what you do and who you are – you want to grow and develop
- If you succeed this time, believe me, next time it will be easier
- Now you are in that positive cycle – anything is possible

> "IF YOU SAY YOU CAN OR YOU CAN'T, YOU ARE RIGHT EITHER WAY."
>
> HENRY FORD

Now, let's link this to you and your team. Your attitude and behaviours affect those of your team. If you are negative then your team will tend to follow your lead. The question, therefore, is what type of people would you like on your bus? Personally, I would like the positive, motivated, 'can-do' type of people; the type who are willing to go that extra mile, who are creative, willing to take a risk, and believe that the team can succeed. **Your role as a leader is to help cement that culture,** to create an environment that supports it, and to lead the team with a positive mindset, attitude, and behaviours to ensure that you all have the very best chance of success.

KEY WORDS IN POSITIVE THINKING

BEHAVIOURS
SELF-BELIEF
CAN DO ATTITUDE
PERSONAL RESPONSIBILITY
BODY LANGUAGE
SUCCESS
RESILIENCE
SELF-AWARENESS
CHOICE
CREATIVITY
CONFIDENCE
ENTHUSIASM

POSITIVE THINKING TIPS FOR THE BUS

- Always look for the positive - if you do, the passengers will
- A positive mindset drives motivation, energy, and 'can do attitude' - what type of bus do you want?
- Remember, you choose your mindset and that impacts the passengers
- For the bus to reach its destination, you need to believe you can succeed
- Mindset drives behaviours - behaviours set the culture of your bus
- When the going gets tough, you need to be able to lead from the front - this is not possible when you are being negative
- Your passengers are more likely to stay on a bus that exudes self-belief and confidence

CHAPTER 13
FEEDBACK

> “FEEDBACK IS THE BREAKFAST OF CHAMPIONS.”
>
> KEN BLANCHARD

Feedback is indeed the breakfast of champions. Speak to anybody who excels at any sport and ask what helped them to reach the top of their game and - more importantly - what kept them there, and you'll find that they seek continuous feedback. Even when they have won, an elite sportsperson will always review what they did well and, of course, what they didn't do so well.

Self-awareness and self-assessment are great, but feedback from others will massively add value to those qualities.

Feedback is about giving and receiving information; information about the perception and opinions of other people on any subject. Some subjects are easier to tackle than others, but I'll come back to that later. First, I'd like to look at some basic rules that should be applied, whatever the nature of the feedback.

It is normally easier (or at least less difficult) to give feedback than to receive it, so let's start with that.

When giving feedback, you must remember:

- Be prepared - don't shoot from the hip
- It must be evidence based
- It is not about the person, it is about the behaviour
- It should be specific and relevant
- It needs to be constructive – to make something better, not make you feel better

- It should be **open, honest and non-judgemental**
- Emotion should be removed before delivery
- You need to think about how you say it – not just what you say
- Ask questions – ensure the recipient has understood exactly what you have said and hasn't taken it out of context
- Listen to their comments

Put simply, all feedback should be planned properly. If you remember the communication process we discussed in Chapter 2, you will know the risks you run if you don't think things through. Often, when we deliver the more **negative** sort of **feedback**, it can go desperately wrong.

Here are a few common reasons for why that can happen:

- We didn't give the recipient opportunity to tell their side of the story
- Issues have been building up, your feedback becomes the last straw and emotions take over, creating a tendency to unload all the other things that have been winding you up for weeks or perhaps months
- It makes us feel better to just get it off our chest - whatever the outcome for the other party

- You haven't given a thought to the outcomes that you would like in return for the feedback
- You haven't given a thought to possible solutions
- Your body language is so out of kilter that you put the other person on the defensive
- You didn't think it through

Giving feedback should be easy if it's done well, especially using the feedback sandwich! Highlight anything positive, then deliver anything that needs changing, and then finish on a high note. Alright, the middle bit can be tricky, but it's just a matter of addressing the behaviour, not the person. Provide evidence, point out your perception of the issue, and suggest something that might work better.

So let's have a look at receiving feedback:

- Perception is reality – just because a person has a different take on a situation, doesn't mean it isn't real in their eyes
- Don't be defensive – constructive feedback is a good thing: this is how we learn and develop
- Don't attempt an alibi and don't blame others – if the feedback is not useful then don't take it onboard. Certainly don't play the victim or try to pass blame over to another

- Listen with an open mind - listen actively and with empathy (the highest level of listening - see Chapter 2). Hear the tone and pitch and pay attention to the body language as well as the words. This will allow you to hear the full message and then make an informed judgement about it

- Don't interrupt - let them finish before making any comment

- Stay objective and keep it in perspective - don't build the feedback into something it isn't. For example, if the feedback is about one piece of work, then it doesn't mean that you're pants at the rest of your job

Without a doubt, receiving feedback is harder – not least because the other person's perception can be mistaken in some way – but we should all be ready to hear feedback when it's offered.

> **Nobody's perfect, not all the time.**

When it comes to the behaviour of leaders, perception might as well be reality because it is other people's perceptions that drive how they react to us. In fact, we should **all** actively be seeking feedback, because that's the very best way to build self-knowledge and self-awareness. We need to strive continuously to be more effective and efficient in everything we do, and feedback allows us to review, to see what's going well, and to decide where we can make positive changes.

Without real feedback from clients, colleagues, and line managers - in fact, anyone relevant - we find ourselves making assumptions about how other people think or feel. While we sometimes have no choice (we cannot always access feedback from them), we can often get their real thoughts if we ask directly in an open, honest and frank manner. There are 3 ways in which to deal with feedback once you've got it:

- Accept it fully - take it onboard because you see the benefit
- Ignore it totally - but only when you have fully listened, reflected and realised that it doesn't add value
- Use what is valuable and ignore what isn't

> **Remember; don't ignore feedback just because you don't like it. Sometimes the toughest feedback is the most valuable.**

Linking this to your role as a leader, feedback is another key ingredient that you can use to build a fully effective team. You should regularly be seeking feedback from your team on how they value your leadership skills, style, approach, etc. Asking questions is the only way to know how successful (or unsuccessful) you are as a leader.

> “THE MORE FEEDBACK YOU GIVE TO PEOPLE, THE BETTER IT IS, AS LONG AS THE FEEDBACK IS OBJECTIVE AND NOT CRITICAL.”
>
> BRIAN TRACY

As I mentioned earlier, there are some subjects about which it is more difficult to give and receive feedback. Reviewing processes, procedures, etc. is not really about you – it's about how many, how much, and what you do. Unfortunately, however, things can get very personal when we start to talk about behaviours.

As such, the key thing to remember is that feedback is never about the person, or about value judgements – it's about behaviour and whether it is effective or appropriate under the circumstances. Let's look at an example scenario:

When an organisation is under pressure, there's always the risk that staff will get defensive about their jobs. This is counter-productive, and especially so at a time when we most need to keep productivity and service levels high. If leaders - **the main drivers of atmosphere** - are also being negative in their behaviours then things are only going to get worse.

When we're under pressure, we tend (naturally enough) to react instinctively and the fight/flight response can kick in. This, in turn, leads to behaviours that others find difficult. It's hard, under those circumstances, to choose rationally and to behave as effectively as we normally would. It's hard even to realise that we are behaving negatively! That's where feedback comes in.

It is your team that will be the first to notice any change in your behaviour. Self-awareness is an early casualty of pressure and if you have an open and honest relationship with your team, you'll have someone to tell you. As leaders, we need to lead by example.

> **We need to set the tone by seeking feedback ourselves and showing that it is a positive thing even if the feedback itself is negative.**

Remember that feedback is something that plays a huge part in leading and developing our team. You should be giving feedback on a regular basis, both positive and negative, as a vital part of the performance management process (Chapter 9). Positive feedback can be a huge motivator: it can make an individual feel valued and build their confidence. On the other side, giving negative feedback can also be a positive experience, but only if you are doing so because you are trying to be helpful, supportive, and are encouraging a change of practice.

KEY WORDS IN FEEDBACK

CONSTRUCTIVE
EVIDENCE
PERSPECTIVE
OPEN
NO BLAME
HONEST
BODY LANGUAGE
ACTIVE LISTENING
CLARITY
ADD VALUE
SPECIFIC
NON-JUDGEMENTAL

FEEDBACK TIPS FOR THE BUS

- So, how effectively are you leading your bus – have you asked?
- Have you given feedback to your passengers? Remember to give both the positive and the negative
- Remember that the atmosphere is affected by behaviours – the most difficult subject on which to give and receive feedback
- Don't shy away from the more difficult feedback – ignoring the negative behaviours will affect other passengers - **that which you permit, you promote**
- When your passengers are trying to give you feedback, ensure that you are actively listening – listen to the NVC

- Only give feedback that will add value to the individual, team, or outcome – it is never delivered for any other reason
- Feedback really will impact in a positive way as your bus journey adapts to the ever changing environment

TICKETS PLEASE

YOUR BUS IS LEAVING THE STATION

Are you ready? Are all of your team onboard, motivated, positive and ready for whatever the journey holds? You've spent your valuable time reading this book, now it's time to see what you can take from it!

I believe that, however effective a team already is, we can always make it better. It's so easy to get complacent just because we are achieving, but if we don't regularly take time out to reflect and review the team's (and your) behaviours and values, they can change without us even noticing.

So have a go now, and answer these questions honestly:

1. Do you need to make any changes or tweaks to create an even more effective team?

2. What's successful? What's not so successful?

3. Do you know what motivates your passengers? Have you asked them?

4. Do you foster an open and honest culture in which everyone can freely express themselves?

5. Have you clearly communicated to the passengers where they are heading? Do they **all** know their fare? Do they understand what they can expect from you and what you expect from them?

6. Have you agreed the standards by which you will work, behave and interact? Are there standards in place that need changing?

Now you've answered these questions, go and ask them of your passengers and see if you get the same answers.

> **Remember, the only way to know how your team feels is to communicate with them.**

If they don't see things the way you do, at least you will know and be able to do something about it.

If you are feeling really courageous, whilst speaking to them add a couple of the questions below to find out how they find your leadership style.

1. What do you do really well as a line manager?

2. What don't you do so well from their perspective?

3. If they could change one thing about you, what would it be?

4. Is there anything more you could do to support them? If so, what?

> **We all have strengths and weaknesses, so encourage openness and honesty.**

Remember the rules of feedback.

I really hope that you have taken something from this book and that it will inspire and motivate you to raise the bar.

> **You lead this team, so please make certain that you lead by example.**

Your people are the most important asset you have, look after them, make them feel valued, celebrate the success, and have some fun!

I wish you every success with all your future journeys.

Sue

ACKNOWLEDGEMENTS

To Terry Van Rhyn, my mentor and friend who has supported me throughout this journey from conception to delivery. Without his unwavering support I would never have reached the final destination. Bill Lawrence, my co-director at TLC, who keeps me grounded, makes sense of my words and stands alongside me through thick and thin. To the staff at Ashgrove Marketing who have offered me their knowledge and expertise, specifically James Dodge for his editing, Graeme on the website, Laura on the marketing, and key to the whole look and feel of the book, Leigh Windell, who I thank for the design and typesetting. To those friends who have lived and breathed this book with me for the 3 years it has taken for me to complete (they know who they are and are too many to list). To Peter Stevens, who allows me the freedom to follow my dreams whilst supporting both Jack and I. To Janet and Kelley at TLC, who are so committed, passionate and enthused in all that we do. To Kate Schofield, my friend, my confidante, my rock, without her support and friendship over the last 40 years this book would never have been possible. Finally, to family, friends, clients and ex- colleagues, you are the ones who gave me the experiences to enable me to write this book.

Thank You

YOUR FEEDBACK

Feedback is at centre of all learning and development, and I would love to hear yours.

If you have any thoughts or comments on **Who's Driving the Bus?**, would like to tell me about your journey, or would like to offer me some advice (or even a little praise!), please feel free to do so by visiting our website.

Sue

www.whosdrivingthebus.net

CONTRIBUTORS

Author – Sue Gee
sue@whosdrivingthebus.net

Art Director - Leigh Windell
loveleighcreates@gmail.com

Editor - James Dodge
james@bluechalkcopy.co.uk

PR and Marketing - Ashgrove Marketing
terry@ashgrovemarketing.com

Web Designer - Graeme Brooks
graeme.brooks@trinity.oxon.org

Leadership and Management Training - TLC
sue@tlc.co.im

Publisher - Ashburton Business Books
james.green@ashburton-publishing.com